Knitted Babes

Claire Garland

MITCHELL BEAZLEY

Knitted Babes

Five Dolls & their Wardrobes to Knit & Stitch

Claire Garland

KNITTED BABES
By Claire Garland

First published in Great Britain in 2005 by
Mitchell Beazley, an imprint of Octopus Publishing Group Ltd,
2–4 Heron Quays, London E14 4JP

ISBN 1 84533 159 1

A CIP record of this book is available from the British Library

Set in Helvetica

Colour origination by Chroma Graphics (Overseas) Pte Ltd, Singapore
Printed and bound in China by Toppan Printing Company Ltd

Senior Executive Editor Anna Sanderson
Executive Art Editor Christine Keilty
Editor Karen Hemingway
Pattern Checker Marilyn Wilson
Photography, Illustration, and Design John Garland
Proofreader Clare Hacking
Indexer Sue Farr
Production Seyhan Esen

Contents

Babes' World 6 • Equipment 8 • Yarn & Fabric 10 • Knitting Know-how 12 • Sewing Know-how 22 • How to Make the Babes 26 • Creating the Look 28 • Completing the Look 30 • Dot Pebbles 32 • Bunny Bright 50 • DD Diva 66 • Flo Tilly 82 • Rudy Ranch 94 • Dolly Bag 108 • Patterns & Templates 110 • Motifs 120 • Knitting Charts 122 • Babes' Care 126

Babes' World

This is an appealing collection of rag dolls, which are modern in approach and retro in feel. They combine the tactile qualities of natural fibres with the versatility of printed textiles – altogether hand-sewn and homespun, to make dolls that are totally unique and charismatic.

All the dolls in the book have winning and individual identities, created by subtle touches to their own delectable wardrobes. This gives each doll a fantastic imaginary lifestyle – really the stuff of dreams.

Each doll, garment, and accessory is small and manageable to make. The dolls themselves are made in stocking stitch, the only other stitch used is garter stitch, and the remaining thing you need to know is how to decrease and increase.

The charm and personality of each lady shines out from the photographs, so any little girl is bound to be drawn to the one that appeals to her most. You, or the child you are knitting for, are sure to find a real favourite.

Equipment

The list of equipment for knitting is short and simple. The principal players are the needles and you only need two sizes – 2³⁄₄mm (US 2) and 3¹⁄₄mm (US 3).

For the knitted projects, you will also need a safety pin for holding stitches that aren't in use; a round-ended needle to sew up the knitted garments and dolls, using the yarn from each project; and scissors for cutting the yarn and loose ends.

The equipment needed for the sewn projects is a basic sewing kit, including pins, needles, sewing thread, and scissors; a sewing machine, if you prefer, although the projects are quite small enough to be sewn by hand; pattern paper for transferring or tracing the patterns and templates provided at the back of the book.

Yarn & Fabric

Most of the yarns for these projects are 4-ply, to suit the petite nature of the garments, and in natural fibres, chosen for their wash and wearability.

Many of the projects are small enough to use up oddments of yarn.

The tension is given for all the knitted projects. Check your tension to make sure that the pattern and size will knit up accurately. Cast on the number of stitches and knit the number of rows advised. If the square measures 10 x 10cm (4 x 4in), your tension is correct. If it is bigger, your knitting is slightly loose, so simply change to a smaller needle. Tension that is slightly too tight will give a smaller square, so change to a larger needle. Keep remaking the square until you have the correct tension.

You will also need scraps of felt and dress fabric in a variety of colours and patterns, as well as buttons, beads, elastic, and all manner of trimmings. Have fun scouring the attic or junk shops, and then chop and change your finds. Scavenge the good parts of old leggings or jeans, or have a go at felting a tired lambswool sweater. Go wild, have fun, and break all the fashion rules!

Knitting Know-how

This section explains all the basic knitting techniques needed for the designs in this book, for the benefit of novice knitters or those who need to refresh their memory. The instructions specific to each design are given within the project and all the knitting patterns appear on pp.122–125. If you want to learn how to knit, work carefully through the steps on the following pages, stay relaxed, and enjoy your creativity.

All the knitting instructions in the book use abbreviated instructions, which are explained in the list below.

ENGLISH-LANGUAGE TERMINOLOGY

UK	USA
Cast off	bind off
Moss stitch	seed stitch
Tension	gauge
Selvedge	selvage
Stocking stitch	stockinette stitch
yf, yo	yarn over

STANDARD ABBREVIATIONS

alt	alternate
beg	beginning
cont	continue
dec	decrease
inc	increase
K	knit
K-wise	knit-wise
M1	make one stitch by working into the back of the loop between the stitch just worked and the next stitch
patt	pattern
P	purl
psso	pass the slipped stitch over
rem	remaining
rep	repeat
skpo	slip a stitch, knit a stitch, pass the slipped stitch over
sl	slip
st(s)	stitch(es)
st st	stocking stitch
tbl	through back of loop
tog	together
yf	bring the yarn forward
yo	bring the yarn over the needle
*	indicates a repeated section, which is explained in the design, e.g. "Repeat from * to end"
(...)	indicates a repeated section, e.g. "(K2tog, yf, K1) twice" means repeat the bracketed instruction twice

HOLDING THE NEEDLES AND WOOL

Knitters hold the needles and wool in various different ways. Try one of these three techniques to see which suits you best. Reverse the instructions if you are left-handed.

English method

While knitting, hold both needles from above between your left thumb, index, and second fingers, leaving the right hand to make the stitches. Hold the yarn on your right hand by passing it under and around the little finger, over the ring finger, under the second finger, and over the index finger. Use your index finger to wind the working yarn over the tip of the needle to make the stitches, while your little finger controls the tension (the tightness/looseness) of the yarn and therefore the neatness of the knitting. As the knitting grows larger, place your thumb under the knitting, holding the needle from below.

Continental method

Hold the needles as you would with the English method only this time wrap the yarn around your left little finger and over the top of the left index finger. Use the right-hand needle to make the stitches, while controlling the tension with your left hand.

French method

Wrap the yarn around your fingers as for the English method but hold the right-hand needle from below as you would a pencil. Use your right index finger to guide the working yarn.

SLIP KNOT

Most knitting starts with a slip knot, which becomes the very first stitch on the needle.

1 Leave a long tail of yarn. Wind the working yarn around your left index finger from front to back and round to the back again. Slide the circle of yarn off the finger and push a loop of working yarn through the circle from back to front. Push the tip of one needle through the loop and pull the slip knot up.

2 Pull the loose tail of yarn down away from the needle to tighten the knot, although not too tightly. Pull the working yarn if you need to slacken the knot.

CASTING ON

There are many methods for casting on and you should use the one you feel most comfortable with for the designs in the book. However the method here gives a strong, neat edge. If you are left handed prop the book up against a mirror and read the diagrams in reverse swapping left for right and vice versa in the text – this rule applies to all the following steps.

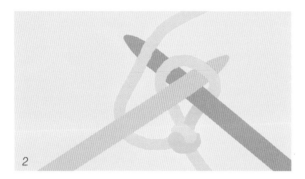

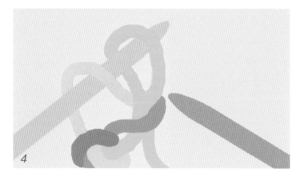

1 Holding the yarn at the back of the left-hand needle, insert the tip of the right hand needle into the slip knot from the front to the back.

2 With the working yarn in your right hand, pass it from the back of the work to the front around the tip of the right-hand needle. (See illustration)

3 With the left-hand needle still in the slip knot, draw the right-hand needle and the working yarn forwards through the slip knot to make a loop on the right-hand needle. (See illustration)

4 Slip the loop onto the left-hand needle and then remove the right-hand needle. You have now cast on two stitches. (See illustration)

To cast on further stitches, insert the right-hand needle into the front of the second stitch and then repeat from step 1. Continue to make stitches in the same way until you have the required number on the needle.

   Now you can begin to knit or purl rows to create the knitted textile.

HOW TO KNIT

A knitted row is usually the right side of the textile. Knitting every row produces garter stitch.

HOW TO PURL

Alternating purled and knitted rows is known as stocking stitch.

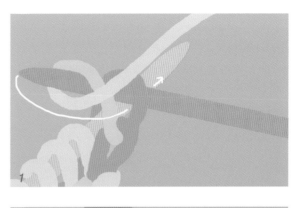

1 With the cast-on stitches on the left-hand needle, insert the tip of the right-hand needle into the first stitch from the front to the back. Hold the yarn as described on p.13 and at the back of the needles. Bring the working yarn around the tip of the right-hand needle, so it is in between the right and left-hand needles.

2 Draw the yarn forwards through the stitch on the left-hand needle making a new stitch on the right-hand needle. Slip the original stitch off the left-hand needle. Continue knitting in this way into each cast-on stitch, until they have all been knitted onto the right needle.

1 Hold the needle with the stitches in your left hand. Bring the working yarn to the front of the work. Insert the right-hand needle through the first stitch on the left-hand needle from the back to the front. Wind the working yarn over the tip of the right-hand needle from the right to the left.

2 Draw the yarn through the stitch on the left-hand needle to make a new stitch on the right-hand needle. Slip the original stitch off the left-hand needle. Continue purling in the same way to the end of the row.

ADDING TEXTURE

Combining knit and purl stitches creates an array of different textures. Here are a couple of examples used in the book and how to achieve them.

Ribbing

Ribbed rows are often used as cuffs, waistbands, and button bands, with occasional use as texture within a garment.

To work K1, P1 rib:

Row 1: Take the yarn to the back of the work and knit one stitch, then bring the yarn to the front of the work and purl one stitch. Repeat these two stitches to the end of the row. The pattern might read: *K1, P1, repeat from * to end of row.

Row 2: Purl one stitch and then knit the next. Repeat these two stitches to the end of the row. The pattern might read: *P1, K1, repeat from * to end of row.

There are other variations, such as K2, P2 rib:

Row 1: *K2, P2, repeat from * to end of row.
Row 2: *P2, K2, repeat from * to end of row.
Note that two knit or two purl stitches are worked together here, creating a double rib pattern.

Moss stitch

This stitch creates a lovely thick texture and can be worked as an alternative to ribbing or as the main textile pattern. Work all the rows in the same way. Knit the first stitch and then purl the second one. Repeat these two stitches to the end of the row. The pattern might read: *K1, P1, repeat from * to end of row.

Note that although the first row looks like the beginning of K1, P1 rib, the subsequent rows offset the knit and purl stitches to create the distinctive texture of moss stitch.

SHAPING

There are a few ways to shape the knitting as you knit. Here are the three methods most suited to the projects in this book.

Turning rows

This method is used to make shapes such as square edges, shoulders, and neck openings. Knit or purl up to where the pattern reads "turn". Then, even if there are still some stitches on the left-hand needle, simply turn the textile over so that the needles are in the opposite hands. Work back along the row you have just created. Then follow the pattern, working on just that section.

Increasing or making stitches

The usual way to add a stitch, especially at the beginning of a row, is to increase one (inc1) or make one (M1) stitch.

1 Work to where the extra stitch is needed. Knit or purl through the front of the stitch but do not drop it off the left-hand needle.

2 With the yarn at the back of the work, slip the tip of the right-hand needle through the back of the stitch still on the left-hand needle, and knit or purl another stitch. Slip the additional stitch off the left-hand needle.

Decreasing stitches

This technique makes the width of the textile narrower and is used for shaping.

On a knit row

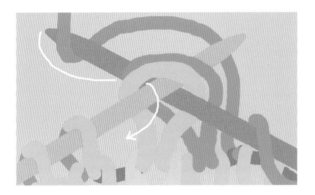

Insert the tip of the right-hand needle from left to right into the second stitch and then the first stitch on the left-hand needle, then knit the two stitches together to make one stitch.

On a purl row

Insert the right-hand needle from right to left through the first two stitches on the left-hand needle, then purl them together to make one stitch.

CASTING OFF

This is the way to finish your piece of knitting so that it does not unravel.

1 Knit or purl the first two stitches according to the pattern, so that both stitches are on the right-hand needle.

2 Use the tip of the left-hand needle to lift the first stitch, illustrated as a white outline, pass it over the second stitch and then off the needle. Knit or purl the next stitch on the left-hand needle. Repeat from the beginning of this step until one stitch remains.

3 Pull the last stitch to lengthen it. Break the working yarn, leaving a long end for sewing up the seams later. Thread the end through the last stitch and pull through to tighten into a knot.

PICKING UP STITCHES

For some designs one part of the garment needs to be knitted onto another that has already been cast off. This technique draws loops through the cast-off edge to create new stitches directly onto the needle.

On a curved, or diagonal edge

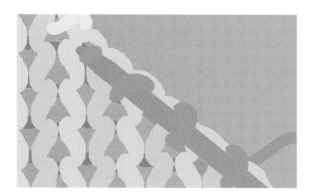

1 Start at the position given in the pattern, such as the front right of a jacket at the cast-on edge, holding the knitted item in your left hand with the right side facing you. Insert the tip of the needle, in your right hand, from the front to the back of the work between the first and second stitches. Wind a new piece of yarn around the needle from back to front, as though knitting a stitch.

2 Draw a loop through the knitting to form a new stitch on the right-hand needle. Continue making new stitches along the edge of the knitting as directed by the pattern until you have picked up the required number of stitches.

On a straight edge

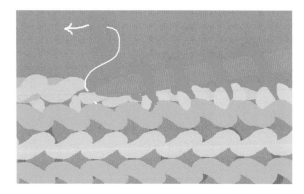

1 Start at the position given in the pattern, such as at the neck edge of a jacket, holding the knitted item in your left hand with the right side facing you. Insert the tip of a knitting needle, in your right hand, from the front to the back of the work through the centre of the first stitch in the cast-off edge. Wind a new piece of yarn around the right-hand needle from back to front, as though knitting a stitch.

2 Draw a loop through the knitting to form a new stitch on the right-hand needle. Continue making new stitches along the edge of the knitting as directed by the pattern until you have picked up the required number of stitches.

SIMPLE SEAMS

When the knitted shapes have been completed they need to be gently pressed and then sewn up to complete the item. Both these methods will be useful for the designs in this book.

Mattress stitch

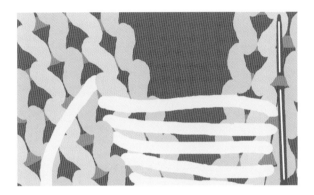

Also known as invisible seaming, this is widely used for joining side and sleeve seams, or where a flat seam with no bulk is required.

1 Place the two pieces to be joined side by side, right sides up, matching stitch for stitch. Thread a knitters' needle with a length of matching yarn.

2 Bring the needle out through the centre of the first stitch, just above the cast-off edge on one piece. Slip the needle through the centre of the corresponding stitch on the other piece and out through the centre of the stitch above. Then insert the needle through the centre of the first stitch on the first piece again and out through the centre of the stitch above it. Continue in this way along the whole seam.

Back stitch

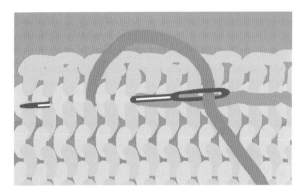

This joining method is used where a firm edge is required to hold the shape of the knitted item.

1 Place the two pieces to be joined right sides facing and pin the edges together, matching stitch for stitch. Thread a knitters' needle as for mattress stitch. Work from right to left. Bring the yarn to the front of the work, one stitch in from both adjacent edges. Take the needle from the front to the back around the cast-on/off edge and back through to the front, one stitch to the left of the original stitch.

2 Take the needle down two stitches to the right, at the end of the previous stitch. Bring the needle up again four stitches to the left. Repeat from the beginning of this step until the seam has been completed along the edge.

Sew in a loose end by threading it onto a needle and working running stitch along the edge of the knitted item. Sew through the bars in between the stitches and oversew the last 2cm (⅜in) to secure the thread.

KNITTING DESIGNS
Here are three techniques to practise adding extra colour detail to your knitting.

Adding on new colours

To add a new colour for a striped pattern, start the new yarn at the beginning of a row. Leaving a long enough end of both the new and the previous yarns to darn in later, simply knot the new yarn to the old one. Slip the knot close to the work before starting to knit or purl the first stitch. When the knitting is complete, weave the ends of yarn in or use them to sew up the seams.

Stranding

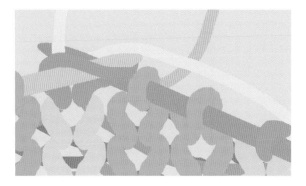

1 To add in new colours following a charted design you will need to strand the yarn across the back of the work. Begin by working with the first colour according to the chart. When you reach the point on the chart where a new colour is indicated, leave the first yarn ball hanging at the back of the work. Start the second colour, leaving a long tail at the back, and work according to the chart. Make sure the tension is not too tight, otherwise the textile will pucker. Join other new colours in the same way.

2 To switch back to a colour used earlier in the row, drop the colour no longer needed and pick up the new colour, taking it over the top of the discarded yarn before working with it.

Swiss darning

This is a simple way to add a pattern over the top of finished stocking stitch. Work from the chart, reading each square as one Swiss-darned stitch. Thread a round-ended sewing needle with the appropriate coloured yarn and bring it up through the middle of a knitted stitch, leaving a long end at the back. Darn an embroidered stitch over the top of each stocking stitch. Weave in all the loose ends.

SPECIAL STITCH TECHNIQUES

Don't be put off by trying to read a pattern through before you start work, especially if knitting patterns are new to you. It's much less daunting to read the pattern as you are knitting, when the instructions will seem much clearer and more straightforward.

However there is nothing daunting about the patterns in this book – they only use two special techniques.

Yo or Yf

This technique can be used as part of the process of creating the eyelets for DD Diva's drawstring bag or the tiny buttonholes for Dot's Blue Bubbles Knit. It creates a small eyelet but, because it doesn't decrease the number of stitches, the hole is closed up again on the return row.

Work up to the point where the pattern reads "yo" or "yf". If you are on a knit row, simply bring the yarn to the front between the needles then take it over the right-hand needle before knitting the next stitch. If you are purling, take the yarn over the right-hand needle then bring the yarn to the front between the needles. Continue working according to the pattern.

Skpo

This is another method for decreasing and shaping a knitted textile to give a fashioned detail and is usually worked on knit rows. It is used on Rudy's Homely Woollen Stole.

1 Work up to the point where the pattern reads "skpo". Slip the next stitch on the left-hand needle onto the right-hand needle without knitting it. Knit the next stitch.

2 Insert the tip of the left-hand needle into the slipped stitch. Then lift the slipped stitch over the knitted stitch and right off the right-hand needle.

Sewing Know-how

All the sewn items in this book take minutes to make and need only the minimal sewing kit. You will find instructions for the few basic stitches and techniques you need on the following pages. The glossary of terms on this page will help you with the instructions in the projects.

TERMINOLOGY

Appliqué	fabric shapes applied by hand or machine to a background fabric
Bias	45-degree angle to the selvedge; fabric is cut on the bias to make bindings and cover fabrics
Binding	narrow bias strip of fabric, either bought ready-made or homemade
Clipping	cutting into a seam allowance to ease the fabric around a curve or cutting across the corner of a seam allowance to reduce bulk
Dots	positional guides, to be transferred from the pattern to the fabric
Fat quarter	A quarter-yard of fabric that measures 45.5 (18in) x approx. 56cm (22in)
Gathering stitch	straight stitch, slightly longer than running stitch and worked by hand or machine; the ends are not secured but drawn up to gather the fabric
Grainline	term referring to the straight grain, which runs lengthwise down the fabric parallel to the selvedge or across the width of the fabric; it is indicated by a long arrow on a pattern and must be correctly aligned on the fabric
Mitre	a diagonal seam joining two pieces of fabric at a corner to reduce bulk on the hemmed edge
Pinking	cutting fabric with zigzag edges to prevent fraying
Pinking shears	zigzag-bladed shears used for pinking edges
Fold line	indicates where the fabric should be folded; sometimes a fold line occurs on the edge of a pattern piece and must be aligned with a fold on the fabric before cutting out, i.e. the pattern shows only half of the complete shape
Quilting	two layers of fabrics sandwiching a layer of wadding and stitched together
Seam allowance	extra fabric needed to make a seam
Selvedge	finished, woven edge of fabric as manufactured
Zigzag stitch	machine stitch used for binding edges on seams or appliqué, or for decoration

TRANSFERRING PATTERNS

The patterns for garment and templates for motifs and other shapes are provided on pp.110–121.

Photocopy the pattern or template, enlarging it if necessary to the size specified. Take a note of how many pieces of fabric you need to cut from each pattern. Pin the pattern pieces to the chosen fabric, taking care to align the grainline arrow with the straight grain of the fabric and, if necessary, place any fold lines on a fold in the fabric. Cut out each shape along the outer line. Transfer any dots, notches, or other markings to the fabric.

MEASURING UP

You may wish to design your own clothes for the dolls. The easiest way to do this is to look at other clothes – turn them inside out to see how they were made and examine the shapes that make up a whole garment.

Replicate the same shapes on paper, scaling them down to suit your doll's measurements. The typical measurements you will need are the circumference of the chest, waist, and head, and the length of the arms and legs – those shown on the photograph are approximate, so make sure to measure your own doll. Add a consistent seam allowance of, say, 6mm (¼in) around each pattern.

SEWING UP

Most of the garments are made using a basic straight-stitch seam. The seam allowance is specified in the project instructions.

Pin the fabric pieces together as specified (usually right sides together). Baste the pieces together if you

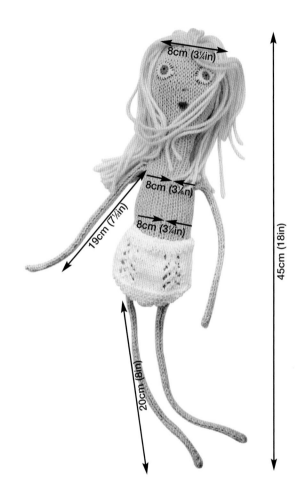

wish, removing the pins. Hand or machine sew along the seam line, using an average size stitch. Remove any basting stitches. Finish the edges of the seams to stop the fabric fraying by either sewing a machine zigzag stitch along the raw edges or pinking the edges with pinking shears.

Press the seam open using a cool iron, unless the pattern directs otherwise.

SEWING STITCHES

Here are instructions for the five basic sewing and embroidery stitches used in the projects.

Slip stitch

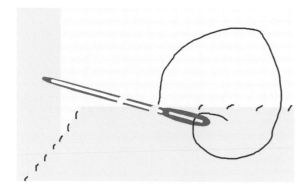

Use this functional stitch to secure two folded edges together, as for a mitred corner, or a folded edge to a flat piece of fabric, as on a hem.

Secure the thread and work from right to left. Bring the needle up through from the flat fabric. Make an almost invisible stitch by picking up a few threads in the fold, then back in through the flat fabric, then out again. Continue to the end of the line.

Making a pocket

Use this method to add a pocket detail on any of the doll's clothes, for example Bunny's Gala Gown. Try patch pockets on trousers or adding a fabric pocket onto a knitted garment. Cut a rectangle of fabric, adding seam allowances. Turn under the raw side and bottom edges. Trim, mitre, and slip stitch the corners on the wrong side. Turn a double hem along the top edge. Mitre the top corners as before.

Pin and baste the pocket in place on the garment, aligning the folded edges with the straight grain of the main garment fabric. Slip stitch the pocket in place, leaving the top edge open.

Running stitch

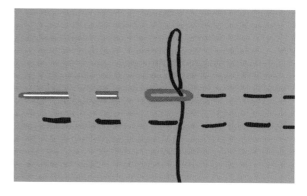

These neat stitches can be used for sewing seams or as a decorative top stitch. Secure the thread and sew small even stitches along the line. The stitches and the gaps should be the same length. For a very secure seam, sew a second line of stitches parallel to the first.

Gathering stitch is sewn in the same way but with longer stitches. Don't secure the thread at either end, use it to gather up the fabric.

Basting stitch

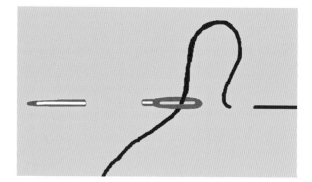

These temporary stitches are designed to hold two pieces of fabric in place until you stitch them together permanently. They are sewn large enough to make pulling them out easy. Work them in the same way as running stitch, but with longer stitches and gaps between.

French knot

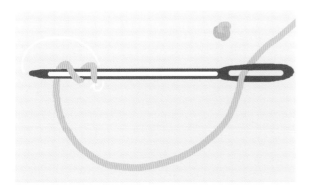

Lying like a bead on the fabric, a French knot is decorative and textural. Bring the needle and thread through to the front. Wind the thread twice around the tip of the needle. Keeping the coils taut, re-insert the needle close to where the thread first emerged. Pull the thread through, making sure the knot holds its shape. Secure the thread at the back.

Buttonhole stitch

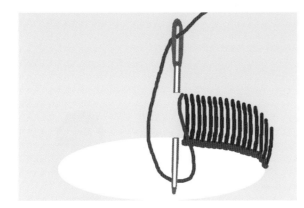

This is worked over raw edges, as for a buttonhole. Secure the thread at one end of the raw edge. Bring the needle to the front at the raw edge. Push the needle through the fabric from the front, about 3mm ($\frac{1}{8}$in) away from the raw edge, to emerge at the raw edge from the back. Loop the working thread around the tip of the needle.

Pull the needle through to tighten the thread along the raw edge. Work along the raw edge, making sure the stitches are evenly spaced. Continue around the end of the slit and then along the other raw edge. Finish by buttonholing across the last end of the slit and securing the thread at the back.

You can also create faux buttonholes by using press studs or touch-and-close tape. Sew the buttons in position on the overlapping fabric. Then sew one half of the press stud or touch-and-close tape on the wrong side, directly beneath each button. Sew the other part of the press stud or tape in corresponding positions on the other half of the garment.

MAKING A CASING
Use this method for creating a casing for elastic or a drawstring, for example around a waist.

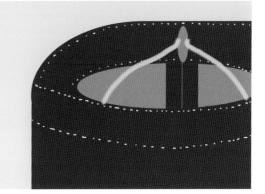

Fold the casing allowance to the wrong side and then fold under the raw edge. Sew the casing in place along both folded edges with running stitch. Leave an opening in the bottom line of stitching or, if the casing runs across a seam, carefully unpick the wrong side of the seam between the two rows of stitches. Thread the elastic or drawstring through the casing, using a safety pin. Join the ends securely and let them slide inside the casing. Slip stitch the casing closed.

How to Make the Babes

MATERIALS 1 x 50g ball of 4-ply yarn in skin colour of choice • Toy stuffing • Yarn for hair in colour of choice • Scraps of felt for eyes and mouth • Sewing thread to match the felt and to work the nose • Pair of 2¾mm (US 2) needles • Round-ended needle for sewing on hair • Embroidery needle for sewing facial features on felt

TENSION 30 sts x 38 rows to 10cm (4in) over st st using 2¾mm (US 2) needles

ABBREVIATIONS *See p.12*

METHOD
Make one back and one front in the same way.
Cast on 18 sts.
Mark 3rd and 16th st to indicate the outside thigh position for each leg.
Work 38 rows in st st beg with a K row.
Dec row: K2tog, K to last 2, K2tog (16 sts).
Next row: P2tog, P to last 2, P2tog (14 sts).
Mark each end to indicate underarm positions.
Cont to dec 1 st at each end of every row until there are 8 sts.
Shape head: Work 3 rows straight in st st.
Inc row: Inc 1 st at each end.
Next row: P.
Rep the last 2 rows until there are 28 sts.
Work 15 rows straight in st st.
Dec row: K2tog all across the row (14 sts).
Next row: P.
Dec row: K2tog all across the row (7 sts).
Cast off.

TO MAKE UP
Sew the back to the front, right sides facing, leaving a gap at the bottom edge for turning.
Turn right sides out. Lightly stuff the shape and oversew the opening to close.

Arms
Cast on 4 sts.
Cont in st st until each arm measures 20cm (8in).
Cast off.
Weave in the loose ends. Sew the cast-on edge of each arm to the body at the underarm markers. The side edges of the arms will be curled in, so there is no need to join them with a seam.

Legs
Cast on 6 sts.
Cont in st st until each leg measures 24cm (9½in). This is the standard length. However, if you wanted to make longer "spaghetti" legs add another 2.5cm (1in) or so (*see* p.89).
Cast off.
Weave in the loose ends. Sew the cast-on edge of each leg to the outside thigh positions on the body. Allow the sides of the legs to curl in the same way as the arms.

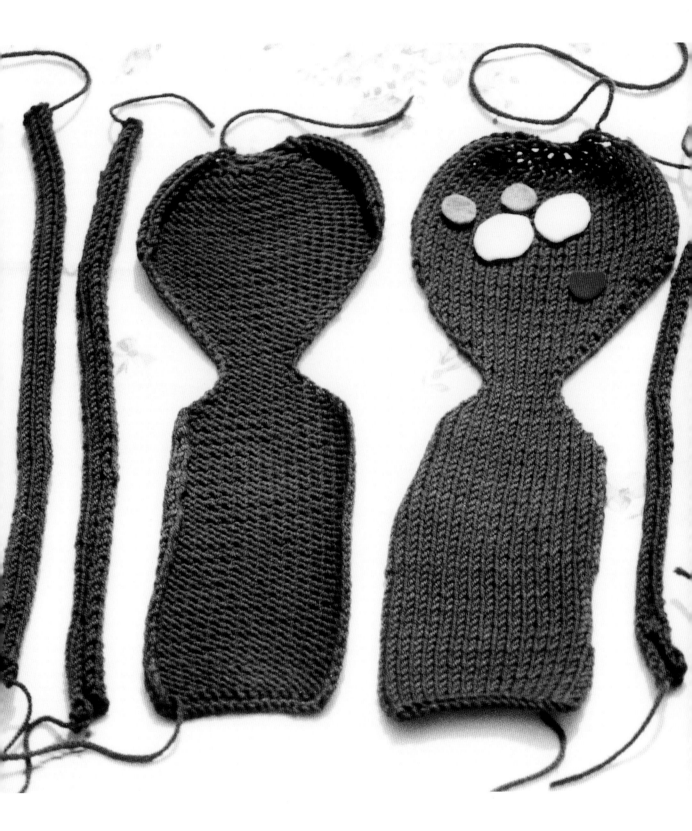

Creating the Look

The look of your babe can be as individual as you are because there are so many ways you can vary the details to give your doll character. Start by creating the facial features.

Templates

The basic templates for the eyes and lips are given on p.114. They can be used same size, or enlarged or reduced on a copier to suit your doll. Cut them out of felt, which is the perfect material – it's easy to cut and sew, and there are so many colours to choose from. Before you cut, make sure the eyes are the same size!

Eyes

Arrange the irises and whites of the eyes on the doll's face and pin them when you are happy with their position. Experiment with placing them closer or wider apart, or even have them at a slight slant. Here are some tried and tested principles that work well: the

outer edges of the eyes should be at least five stitches away from the sides of the head and nine stitches away from the crown.

To sew on the eyes, use a double strand of thread in black to create the pupil. Secure the thread at the back of the eye white. Take the needle through the centre of the eye white and the iris. Stitch a french knot or a few straight stitches to make the pupil.

Alternatively, you could use a small circle of black felt for larger pupils and glue the parts of the eye together with fabric adhesive. If you wish, sew straight stitches radiating around the iris onto the white in a colour to match or contrast with the iris.

Attach each eye to the doll's face with straight stitches in your chosen colour, radiating around the eye white to give the impression of eyelashes.

Lips

Sew the lips in place by working tiny stitches across the lips in a matching shade of thread to the felt. The position of the stitching and even extending the stitches beyond the felt will give your doll an individual look, so experiment with different pouts and smiles.

Finishing touches

Give your doll a cute nose by making a few stitches in the same colour as the lips across one or two of the knitted stitches.

Finally, if you wish, add freckles or beauty spots to the face by working a light dusting of French knots.

Completing the Look

Once you have designed your babe's face, you may know exactly how you want to colour and style her hair. If not, here are a few ideas.

You and your child can have hours of fun choosing the yarn for the doll's hair. You can use all sorts. Mohair yarn will create a wonderful head of fluffy fairy hair, while an unravelled jumper will give you marvellous curls, or, alternatively, twist a thick yarn around your finger into coils then, when the coils have been slipped off your finger, gently steam. Style the hair by cutting a cheeky fringe or a sleek bob. Plait or bunch longer hair or twist it into a very sophisticated chignon.

You can adorn the hair with ribbons, scrunchies, felt flowers, or a hair band. Thread beads onto the ends of single strands or whole plaits. In short, the options are endless and you can be a perpetual hairdresser!

Prepare the hair as a single piece before attaching it to the head. First cut strands of yarn slightly longer than double the desired length – you can always trim later. Group the strands into bundles, matching the ends. Use the same coloured thread in a large-eyed sharp needle. Securely sew the centre of each bundle to the centre of the next bundle.

When all the hair is sewn together, place it on the head and sew it securely along the centre of the head, starting at the front and finishing at the back. Then – go style!

SAFETY NOTE

It is imperative to keep the safety of young children in mind when making these dolls. Sew seams and attach trimmings securely. Don't attach small, hard embellishments such as buttons and beads, or use fluffy yarn such as mohair on dolls for children under three years old. Use washable stuffing that conforms to safety standards, and take great care to remove all pins, needles, and loose threads.

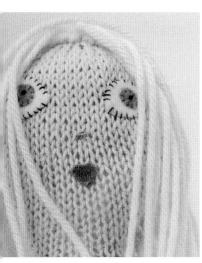

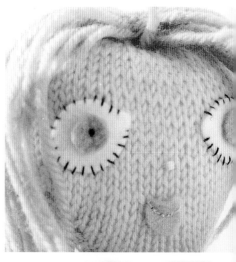

Dot Pebbles

This petite, totally cool, sun, sand, and surf chick is a regular water babe. Dot is vivacious and breezy, always on the go. She spends all her days on the beach, catching rays when the sun shines – and it shines all the time, of course! Her clothes have to reflect this free, summer lifestyle – relaxed yet fitted for active play, layered to suit the climate. They're totally cool and a little bit retro, and as easy as proverbial pie. So-oo today! Everyone loves gorgeous little Dot.

Beach Gear Sleeveless Seersucker Blouse • Board Cords and
Sand Slides • Blue Bubbles Knit • Lifesaver Bather • Dot 4 T • Retro Beachbag
• Floral Swim Hat • Go Speedy Swimsuit Set • Knitted Rubber Duck Ring
• Striped Slip-on Dress

Sleeveless Seersucker Blouse

Cool textural garment with miniature buttons

WHAT YOU NEED Fat quarter of seersucker fabric • 2 tiny buttons taken from old dolls' clothes or similar • 2 press studs • Basic sewing kit • Pattern paper

NOTE All seams are 6mm (¼in) wide and stitched with right sides facing unless stated otherwise.

METHOD

1 Photocopy or transfer at 100 per cent the pattern on p.118. Fold the fabric in half and pin the pattern pieces as detailed on p.23. Cut out all the pieces as directed and transfer the pattern markings to the fabric.

2 Fold the opening edges of both front pieces to the wrong side, along the fold lines. Turn in a 3mm (⅛in) seam along both raw edges. Press, then sew both hems in place.

3 Sew both front pieces to the back piece along the shoulder seams. Press.

4 Pin one collar piece to a collar stand, right sides facing, matching the dots and the long edges between the dots. Sew the seam and press open. Repeat, to join the other collar and collar stand.

5 Pin the two collars right sides facing. Sew them together from the neck edge on the collar stand, around the three straight edges of the collar, and to the other end of the neck edge on the stand. Trim the corners and turn the whole collar right sides out. Press the seams. Press.

6 Press under a 6mm (¼in) turning along the neck edge of both collar stands. Slip stitch the right side of one collar stand to the wrong side of the neck of the blouse. Top stitch along the edge of the other collar stand, attaching it to the right side of the neck edge and concealing the raw edges. Top stitch, 3mm (⅛in) from the outer edges of the collar. Press.

7 Make two vertical buttonholes, spacing them evenly down the right front. Sew two buttons onto the left front to correspond with the button holes (for more detail, *see* p.25).

8 Turn under a double 3mm (⅛in) hem around the arm holes and sew in place.

9 Fold under a double 3mm (⅛in) hem around the bottom edge of the blouse and sew in place. Press.

To make Dot's bandanna, simply cut a 30cm (12in) square from a scrap of suitably retro fabric and then sew a line of running stitch 5mm (⅛in) from the edges. Fray the edges up to the stitch lines.

Fold the bandanna in half diagonally and then tie at the back of Dot's head.

Board Cords and Sand Slides

Hipster cords with polka-dot skirt, teamed with beachy slides

WHAT YOU NEED FOR CORDS

Worn-out cords or fat quarter of baby cord •
28 x 5cm (11 x 2in) vintage or retro-patterned
fabric for the skirt • Scrap of felt for the star
motif • 6mm- (¼in-) wide elastic • Basic
sewing kit • Pattern paper • Safety pin

NOTE All seams are 6mm (¼in) wide
and stitched with right sides facing unless
stated otherwise.

METHOD

1 Fray one long edge of the skirt panel
   to make a 6mm (¼in) fringe.
2 Enlarge the trouser pattern on p.111 to
   167 per cent. Fold the trouser fabric and
   pin the pattern pieces as detailed on p.23.
   Cut out all the pieces.
3 Press under a 6mm (¼in) turning along
   the long unfrayed edge of the skirt. Sew
   together the side seam. Turn the skirt
   right side out.
4 Sew each trouser front to the matching
   trouser back, along the outside and
   inside leg seams.
5 Turn one leg right side out and slip it
   inside the other leg, right sides facing.
   Matching the waist edges and inside
   leg seams, stitch the legs together
   along the centre front and back seams.
   Turn right sides out.

6 Fold a 10mm (⅜in) turning to the right side
   around the waist edge of the trousers.
   Match the wrong side of the skirt to the
   right side of the trousers, aligning the top
   edges. Sew around the top edge, close
   to the folds. Sew another row of stitches
   6mm (¼in) down from the first, leaving an
   opening for elastic. Cut elastic to fit the
   waist and, using a safety pin, thread it
   through the casing. Join the ends
   securely and sew the opening closed.
7 Using the template on p.121, cut a star
   motif out of felt. Attach it with running
   stitch near the bottom edge of one
   trouser leg. Fray the bottom edges
   of the trousers. Press.

WHAT YOU NEED FOR SLIDES

Scraps of 4-ply yarn • Pair 2¾mm (US 2)
needles • Round-ended needle

METHOD

Make two the same.

Cast on 14 sts for the sole. Work 22
rows in garter st. Cast off, then fold the
strip into thirds and sew up the side seam.

Make the strap by casting on 3 sts in a
contrasting colour. Work 14 rows in garter
st. Cast off. Finally, attach the ends of
each strap to the opposite sides of each
sandal sole.

Blue Bubbles Knit

Contrast-edged cardigan with bubble pattern detail

WHAT YOU NEED 1 x 50g ball of 4-ply yarn in blue (M) • Scraps of 4-ply yarn in brown, pink, and white • Pair 2³⁄₄mm (US 2) needles • 2 x 1cm (⅜in) diameter buttons • Safety pin • Round-ended needle

TENSION 30 sts x 38 rows to 10cm (4in) over st st using 2³⁄₄mm (US 2) needles

ABBREVIATIONS *See p.12*

CHART NOTE Enlarge the chart on p.124 on a photocopier for ease of reading. Read it from right to left on odd-numbered (K) rows and from left to right on even (P) rows, stranding the yarn at the back of the work.

METHOD

Back

Using yarn B, cast on 31 sts. Work in simple rib as follows:

Row 1: K1, *P1, K1; rep from * to end.
Row 2: P1, *K1, P1; rep from * to end.
Rep last 2 rows once more.
Change to M. Beg with a K row, work in st st for 14 rows.
Shape armholes: Cast off 2 sts from beg of next 2 rows (27 sts).
Fashion armholes: K3, K2tog, K to last 5 sts, K2tog, K3 (25 sts).

Next row: P.
Rep last 2 rows until there are 21 sts.
Work 7 rows straight.
Shape shoulders: Cast off 5 sts at beg of next 2 rows. Leave rem 11 sts on a safety pin.

Left front

Using yarn B, cast on 16 sts. Work 4 rows in rib as follows:
*K1, P1, rep from * to end.
Change to M and cont in st st for 8 rows**.
St st a further 6 rows.
Shape armholes: Cast off 2 sts. K to end.
Next row: P.
Fashion armholes: K3, K2tog, K to end (13 sts).
Rep last 2 rows until there are 12 sts.
Next row: P.
Shape neck: ***K3, K2tog, K to last 5 sts, K2tog, K3 (10 sts).
Next row: P3, P2tog, P to end.
Next row: K to last 5 sts, K2tog, K3.
Rep last 2 rows until 5 sts rem.
St st 2 rows ending at armhole edge.
Cast off.

Right front

Work as for left front up to**.
Next row: K7, change to patt colour W and K2. Change to M and K to end.

Cont to follow patt from chart on p.124, taking note of shapings as follows:

Shape armhole: Cast off 2 sts, P to end.

Next row: K to last 5, K2tog, K3 (13 sts).

Next row: P.

Cont to dec in this way until there are 12 sts, ending on a P row.

Shape neck: As left front from *** to end, reversing shapings.

Sleeves

Make two similar with the exception of working the bubble pattern on one.

With B, cast on 29 sts. Work 4 rows in simple rib as back.

Change to M. Beg with K row, work in st st for 33 rows.

Shapings: Cast off 2 sts from beg of next 2 rows (25 sts).

Next row: P3, P2tog, P to last 5 sts, P2tog, P3 (23 sts).

Next row: K.

Rep last 2 rows twice more (19 sts).

Next row: P3, P2tog, purl to last 5 sts, P2tog, P3 (17 sts).

Cast off 3 sts from beg of every row until 5 sts rem. Cast off.

Join shoulder seams.

Buttonhole band

With right side of the knitting facing, pick up and K: 27 sts up right front, 11 sts on safety pin, 27 sts down left front.

Work one row simple rib.

Next row: Work two buttonholes as follows: Rib 4, *yo, P2tog, rib 8, rep from * once more, rib to end.

Work one more row simple rib. Cast off.

Sew on buttons to match buttonholes.

TO MAKE UP

Sew in all the ends. Very lightly steam the knitting flat. Join the side and sleeve seams and sew the sleeves into the armholes.

Lifesaver Bather

A fun item, fashioned somewhere between a wet suit and an all-in-one swimsuit.

WHAT YOU NEED 1 x 50g ball of 4-ply yarn in red (M) • Scraps of 4-ply yarn in white and blue • Pair 2¾mm (US 2) needles • Safety pin • Round-ended needle

TENSION 30 sts x 38 rows to 10cm (4in) over st st using 2¾mm (US 2) needles

ABBREVIATIONS *See p.12*

CHART NOTE Enlarge the chart on p.123 on a photocopier for ease of reading. Read it from right to left on odd-numbered (K) rows and left to right on even (P) rows, stranding the yarn at the back of the work.

METHOD

Starting at the **front** right leg and M, cast on 13 sts. Work in rib as follows:

**Row 1: K1, *P1, K1; rep from * to end.
Row 2: P1, *K1, P1; rep from * to end.
Rep last 2 rows once more.
Next row: Beg with K row, work in st st for 8 rows**. Cast on 2 sts. Break yarn and leave sts on a safety pin.
Front left leg: Cast on 13 sts and work as right leg from **.
Next row: K13, K across 15 sts on the safety pin (28 sts).

Work st st for 9 rows***.
Pattern: Work in patt over the next 22 rows of st st.
Shape armholes: Dec 1 st at each end of this K row.
Next row: P.
Next row: K2tog, K to last 2 sts, K2tog (24 sts).
Next row: P.
Next row: K.
Next row: P2tog, P to last 2 sts, P2tog.
Next row: K.
Rep last 2 rows twice more (18 sts).
Next row: P2tog, P to last 2 sts, P2tog (16 sts).
Shape shoulder straps: K2tog, K3, turn and work on these 4 sts for left shoulder strap. St st 26 rows. Cast off.
Rejoin yarn at inside edge, cast off 6, K to last 2 sts, K2tog. Continue to work in st st to match other strap.

Back

Work as for front right leg and front left leg up to ***. Cont in st st for another 15 rows.
Shape back: P8, turn and work on these sts only.
Next row: (K2tog) twice, K to end.

Next row: P.

Rep last 2 rows twice more.

Cast off 2 rem sts.

Rejoin yarn to rem 20 sts.

Cast off 12 sts, P to end.

Next row: K to last 4 sts, (K2tog) twice.

Next row: P.

Rep last 2 rows twice more.

Cast off.

TO MAKE UP

Sew in all the ends. Gently steam the knitting flat. Join the side and inside leg seams. Cross the straps at the back and attach the cast-off ends to the waist edge, 2.5cm (1in) in from the side seams.

This bather is open to many interpretations. The version on the front cover is worked using the same pattern, but without the lifesaver detailing. You could try working a stripy pattern, alternating garter and stocking stitch for each striped band – there are many patterns and colours with which you could design your own bather.

Have a go and throw up a few surprises along the way!

Extra Babe Things

This little t-shirt is made from scraps of worn-out kids' t-shirts, patched together.

To make the "Dot 4" t-shirt, seek out scraps of old jersey t-shirt to make two 12.5cm (5in) squares and two 6cm (2½in) squares, either as whole pieces or patched together. Make templates at 100 per cent from p.119 and cut out the fabric shapes. Fold a sleeve, right sides together, and sew a 3mm (⅛in) seam along the long side. Turn under and sew a small hem at the cuff. Turn right side out. Repeat for the other sleeve.

Turn under and sew a 6mm (¼in) hem around the neckline of the back and front pieces. Press along the fold lines at the shoulders. Place the pieces right sides together and, leaving openings for the sleeves, sew 6mm (¼in) seams up the sides. Turn right sides out. Insert the sleeves and sew them into position. Hem the bottom edge. Embroider the doll's name onto a scrap of jersey and sew it in place on the front of the t-shirt.

Choosing the right buttons, fabrics, and trimmings for the garments and the best colours for the doll is rather like choosing clothes for yourself or your children – they really are essential to the overall look and feel.

Personalizing garments, such as the "Dot 4" t-shirt, and making fun accessories like the rubber duck ring helps to give each doll her very individual look.

When choosing buttons, look for old dolls' and baby clothes. Also pick up old containers of buttons or beads from junk shops and rummage sales – they were once carefully removed from garments past their best and deserve to be given a new lease of life.

Make this tiny bag in minutes out of scraps of retro-patterned curtain or dress fabric. Add simple detail with a frayed square of different fabric.

To make the bag, cut 24 x 12cm (9½ x 4¾in) of the main fabric. Press 5mm (³⁄₁₆in) to the wrong side along one long edge. Fold over a further 5cm (2in) to make a drawstring casing and sew in place. At each end of the casing, turn under and sew a 6mm (¼in) hem.

Fold the fabric in half lengthways, right sides together, and press. Open it out and sew a square scrap of different fabric, frayed around the edges, on the front of the bag fabric.

Fold the bag fabric in half again and sew along the side and base edges. Turn the bag right side out and thread a length of cord through the drawstring casing.

To make a towel to go in the bag, simply knit a 10cm (4in) square in 4-ply, working garter stitch. Add a fringe to opposite ends.

Accessories for your doll can be quick, easy, and fun to design and make. This swim hat is adapted from the knitted hats.

To make the swim hat, knit the crown as for the hat on p.55. To make a strap, cast on 20 sts. Knit two rows. Cast off. Repeat for the second strap and attach one end of each strap to opposite sides of the hat.

Cut out 15 felt flowers, at 100 per cent, from the motif on p.12. Attach them securely to the hat by sewing one stitch in the centre of each flower.

Go Speedy Swimsuit Set

Swimsuit with go-faster stripes and matching duck ring

WHAT YOU NEED FOR SWIMSUIT

Small amounts of 4-ply yarn in lilac (L), yellow (Y), and turquoise (T) • Pair of 2¾mm (US 2) needles • Round-ended needle

TENSION 28 sts x 48 rows to 10cm (4in) over garter st using 2¾mm (US 2) needles

ABBREVIATIONS *See p.12*

METHOD

Work the back and front the same. Start at the gusset with L. Cast on 6 sts. K 1 row.
Inc row: K1, M1, K to last st, M1, K1.
Rep the last row until there are 26 sts.
Change to Y, K 2 rows.
Change back to L, K 2 rows.
Change back to Y, K 14 rows.
Next row: Change to T, and K.
Next row: Purl. Cont in st st for 6 more rows ending on a P row.
Shoulder straps: Cast off 3 sts. K3 inlcuding stitch used to cast off. Turn and work st st for 22 rows. Cast off.
Rejoin yarn. Cast off 14, K to end.
Next row: Cast off 3 sts. P to end and cont in st st to match the other strap. Cast off.

TO MAKE UP

Join the cast-on edges at the gusset. Sew up the side and shoulder seams.

WHAT YOU NEED FOR DUCK RING

Small amounts of 4 ply in yellow (Y) and beige (B) • Pair of 2¾mm (US 2) needles • Scrap of yellow felt • Black thread • Pattern paper • Toy stuffing

TENSION 28 sts x 48 rows to 10cm (4in) over garter st using 2¾mm (US 2) needles

METHOD

Ring: Cast on 20 sts in Y. Garter st until the work measures 28cm (11in). Cast off.
Duck's head: Starting at the bill end with B, cast on 8 sts in B.
Next row: Inc K-wise into every st (16 sts). Beg with a P row, st st 11 rows.
Next row: (K2tog) 3 times, inc into next 4 sts, (K2tog) 3 times (14 sts).
P 1 row. St st 5 more rows. Cast off.

TO MAKE UP

Fold the ring in half lengthways and sew up the long seam. Firmly stuff the ring and then sew the two ends together.

Cut out two felt duck's bills, using the template on p.113. Sew them to the cast-on edge. Embroider two eyes on the head.

Sew the cast-on and cast-off edges of the ring together. Sew up the side edges, leaving an opening. Stuff the head and sew up the opening. Attach the head to the ring.

Striped Slip-on Dress

Easy wear doesn't come much easier than this casual cap-sleeved sundress. Chill out!

WHAT YOU NEED 1 x 50g ball of 4-ply cotton yarn in turquoise (T) • 1 x 50g ball of 4-ply cotton yarn in gold (G) • Pair 3¼mm (US 3) needles • Round-ended needle

TENSION 23 sts x 32 rows to 10cm (4in) over garter st using 3¼mm (US 3) needles

ABBREVIATIONS *See* p.12

METHOD

Knit in one piece. Using T, cast on 70 sts. Work 2 rows in garter st.

Rows 3 & 4: Change to G. Rep last 2 rows.

Rep last 4 rows, forming striped patt, for 22 more rows.

Row 27: K.

Dec row: K2, *K2tog, rep from * to last 2 sts, K2 (37 sts).

Next row: K.

Dec row: K1, *K2tog, rep from * to end (19 sts).

Knit 9 rows in stripe patt.

Shape back waist: Cast off 2 sts, K to last 2 sts, cast off 2 sts.

Rejoin yarn to centre 15 sts and K 10 rows in patt.

Shape strap: K4, cast off 7 sts, K to end.

Cont on last 4 sts and K 12 rows.

Next row: Dec 1 st at each end (2 sts). K 2 rows. Cast off.

Rejoin yarn to rem 4 sts at neck edge and work right strap to match.

TO MAKE UP

Sew up the back seam. Sew the ends of the straps to the edge of the waist at the back.

Try different colour combinations for striking effects. There's no need to stick to just two colours – you could go for psychedelic vibrancy. Clash colours or contrast them – Dot could have a different dress for every day of the week!

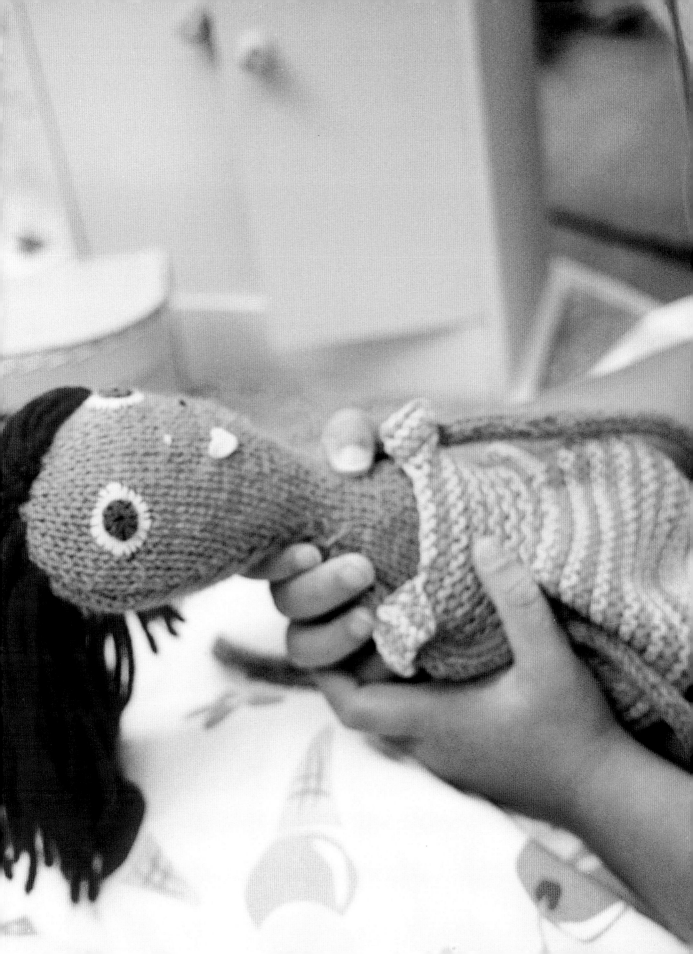

Bunny Bright

An ethereal, sweet-natured beauty, BB also has a sweet tooth and a penchant for ice-cream sodas. She's a café-bar star – cappuccinos, sodas, and sorbets are her lifestyle. Bunny has a voracious appetite for glamorous movie-star frocks and gowns. But however fluffy and floaty her style may be, she always remains a devoted friend.

Frock Shop
Gingham Gala Gown with Ascot Hat • Pink Knit Sac • Butterfly Mules • Sparkly Ribbon-tied Gown • Flower Power Mini • Funky Psychedelic A-line • Lacy Knickers • Sequin Bag • Flip Flops • 50s-style Bag • Two-tone Mules • Yellow Mules • Dolly Bag • Retro Pink Floral Polo Knit

Gingham Gala Gown with Ascot Hat

Elegant long dress with cross-stitch detail, a felted flower corsage, and special-occasion hat

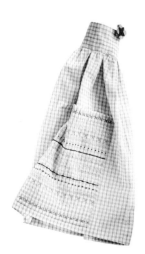

WHAT YOU NEED FOR THE GOWN

30cm (⅓yd) gingham fabric • Hooks and eyes • Scraps of felt • Basic sewing kit • Embroidery silks (optional)

NOTE All seams are 6mm (¼in) wide and stitched with right sides facing unless stated otherwise.

METHOD

1 Begin by making the bodice. Cut a strip of gingham, measuring 10 x 8cm (4 x 3¼in). Fold it in half lengthways, aligning the edges. Sew a seam along each short end. Press the seams open. Turn the band right side out. Press. Sew hook and eyes, equally spaced, on the two short edges, which form the back of the bodice.

2 Cut a strip of gingham measuring 20 x 5cm (8 x 2in) for the shawl and make it in the same way as the bodice, without the hooks and eyes.

3 To make the skirt, cut a 30 x 25cm (12 x 10in) rectangle of gingham. Sew a seam to join the two short ends. Press the seam open.

4 Run a gathering stitch around the waist edge and draw up the thread so the skirt matches the bottom of the bodice.

5 Sew the gathered waist to the bodice, matching the back seam to the back edges of the bodice.

6 Turn and sew a double 6mm (¼in) hem around the bottom edge of the skirt.

7 Cut the felt corsage using the flower template on p.121. Sew it in place.

8 Attach a pocket to the skirt, following the instructions on p.24. Embroider it first, following the photograph, if you wish.

9 Use a few discreet stitches to attach the shawl to the back of the bodice. When the dress is on the doll, sweep the shawl over both shoulders and secure with a loose knot at the back.

You could also adapt the dress by making small sleeves from narrow bands of gingham or straps of rickrack or ribbon. Before attaching them permanently, adjust them for the best position while the dress is on the doll.

WHAT YOU NEED FOR THE HAT

About half a ball of 4-ply yarn • Pair 2¾mm
(US 2) needles • Round-ended needle

METHOD

Crown

Cast on 17 sts. K 5 rows.

Next row: Dec 1 st at each end.

Rep the last 6 rows once more. K 3 rows.

Next row: Dec 1 st at each end.

Rep the last 4 rows until 5 sts rem.

Next row: Dec 1 st at each end. Cast off.

Make another 3 pieces the same.

Join the four pieces leaving the cast on
edges open.

Hat brim

Cast on 7 sts. K 2 rows.

Next 2 rows: K5, turn, k back.

Rep the last 4 rows until the shorter edge
of the brim fits along the cast on edges of
the crown. Cast off.

TO MAKE UP

Join ends neatly then sew the brim to the
hat. Add floral corsages or, for a temporary
effect, real flowers.

Extra Babe Things

This pink bag is knitted in one piece in garter stitch and lined in a contrasting fabric.

Cast on 20 sts. Cont in garter st. Knit the first row. Then inc 1 st into the first and last st on the next and every 6th row, until there are 28 sts on the needle. Cast off.

Fold the bag in half lengthways across the cast-on and cast-off edges. Sew up the back seam. Position the seam so it is centred at the back of the bag. Sew along the cast-on edge. Turn the bag inside out.

Make a bag of similar dimensions from a pretty, contrasting fabric. Turn under the top edge. Slip the fabric bag over the knitted bag, wrong sides facing, and hand sew in place. Turn the bag right sides out.

Make a twisted cord out of two 15cm (6in) lengths of yarn. Knot the ends and sew one end to each side of the bag.

Let your children join in the fun by helping with the doll's accessories.

Children love to thread beads and can do so very successfully from quite a young age. It helps to develop hand-eye co-ordination and – if they know that they are helping you – gives quite a sense of achievement.

Tie a bead onto one end of a length of fine elastic and ask them to thread it with beads. Let them have the run of the bead tin to create their own string of pearls, plastic gems, or sparkly faux jewels. Sharing quiet moments like these is a real pleasure!

No gown is complete without a Cinderella slipper. Even a knitted one can be just as elegant as glass, and equally suitable for a princess.

Tension Using 4-ply yarn; 30 sts x 38 rows to 10cm (4in) over st st using 2¾mm (US 2) needles

Slipper sole: Cast on 8 sts. St st 14 rows. Cast off.

Slipper upper: Beg at the toe end, cast on 3 sts.

Row 1: K.

Next row: Knit, inc in every st (6 sts). Rep the last 2 rows once (12 sts). K 5 more rows. Cast off.

To make up: Press each sole flat and fold it lengthways, purl sides facing. Oversew the edges and place the seam under the sole. Oversew the cast-on edge, to make the toe of the slipper. Oversew the cast-off edge to make the heel end. Shape the slipper upper over the tip of your index finger. Then lay it over the toe end and sew it in place. Sew on a felt butterfly using the motif on p.120.

Satin ribbons are a luxury addition to Bunny's or any of the other dolls' wardrobes.

Be exuberant with your trimmings and bows. These dolls, and the children they are made for, love elaborate glittery and ribbony things to handle and tie.

However, caution is needed. You must attach small embellishments very securely and they should not be used at all on dolls for children under 3 years old.

Sparkly Ribbon-tied Gown and Flower Power Mini

50s-style satin and florals sundress with fitted bodice

WHAT YOU NEED For both: Fabric for the upper bodice, lining, and skirt • Ribbons • Braid • Basic sewing kit • Pattern paper For the mini: Bias binding for the armhole trim • 2 buttons

NOTE All seams are 6mm (¼in) wide and stitched with right sides facing unless stated otherwise.

LONG GOWN METHOD

1 Enlarge the template for the bodice front on p.110 to 143 per cent. Cut one for the bodice and one for the lining.

2 Cut four 10cm (4in) lengths of ribbon. Pin two ribbons to each shoulder of the bodice, matching raw edges.

3 Sew the lining to the bodice front along the neck, shoulders (securing the ribbons), and side seams. Trim the corners and turn right sides out. Press.

4 To make the skirt, cut a 30 x 25cm (12 x 10in) rectangle of fabric. Fold it widthways, align the short edges, and sew up the back seam. Press the seam.

5 Run a gathering stitch around the waist edge and draw up the thread to fit twice the width of the bodice. Sew the bodice

to the gathered waist edge, aligning the back seam to the back of the dress. Turn up a double 6mm (¼in) hem along the bottom edge. Trim the waist line with ribbon or braid.

MINI METHOD

1 Using the template on p.110, cut out two bodice and two lining shapes. Sew the two bodice pieces together at the shoulder and side seams. Press. Repeat for the linings. Sew the lining to the bodice around the neckline. Clip into the curves and turn right sides out. Press.

2 For the skirt, cut a 15 x 23cm (6 x 9in) piece of the same fabric. Gather the waist edge to fit the bodice. Complete the skirt as for the long gown.

3 Attach the bias binding around the armholes, right sides facing, starting and finishing neatly at the side seams. Slip stitch the other edge of the binding in place on the lining side of the bodice.

4 Turn in and sew the open back edges. Make two buttonholes on the right back and sew two buttons on the left back. Sew braid or ribbon around the waist, leaving a length to tie at the back.

Funky Psychedelic A-Line

Really, really retro revival raver with frilly tennis knickers

WHAT YOU NEED FOR THE DRESS

Fat quarter of 70s-style fabric • Scraps of matching fabric for lining • Basic sewing kit • Pattern paper

NOTE All seams are 6mm (¼in) wide and stitched with right sides facing unless stated otherwise.

METHOD

1 Enlarge the pattern on pp.116–17 to 143 per cent. Cut the two dress pieces from the main fabric and the two bodice pieces from the lining.

2 Sew the linings to the bodice fronts and backs around the neck line, back opening, and armholes. Clip into the curves and turn right sides out. Press.

3 Sew together the shoulder and side seams of the main dress. Press seams open. Fold under the same seams on the lining and slip stitch in place. Press.

4 Turn and sew a double 3mm (⅛in) hem around the bottom edge of the dress.

To make a headband, cut a 15 x 4cm (6 x 1½in) piece of the dress fabric. Fold it in half lengthways, right sides facing. Sew around the edges, leaving an opening for turning. Trim the corners and turn out right sides out. Press. Oversew the opening.

WHAT YOU NEED FOR KNICKERS

1 x 50g ball of 4-ply cotton yarn in white • Pair of 2¾mm (US 2) needles • 20cm (8in) shirring elastic

TENSION 30 sts x 38 rows to 10cm (4in) over garter st using 2¾mm (US 2) needles

ABBREVIATIONS *See* p.12

METHOD

Work the back and front alike. Beg at the gusset, cast on 6 sts. K 2 rows.
Next row: K1, yf, K to last st, yf, K1.
Rep the last row until there are 28 sts.
Cont 4-row patt as follows:
1st row: K5, yf, K2tog, K1, K2tog, yf, K8, yf, K2tog, K1, K2tog, yf, K to the end.
2nd row: P.
3rd row: K6, yf, sl1, K2tog, psso, yf, K10, yf, sl1, K2tog, psso, yf, K to the end.
4th row: P.
Cont in patt until work measures 6.5cm (2½in) from the cast-on edge.
Rib: *K1, P1, rep from * to end.
Rep the last row 3 times more. Cast off.

TO MAKE UP

Oversew the cast-on edges at the gusset. Join the side seams. Thread shirring elastic through the ribbing at the waist.

Essential Accessories

All the accessories in this section can be made within a couple of hours to complement the wardrobe of any of the babes.

Note All the templates are on pp.114–15. All seams are 6mm (¼in) width and stitched right sides facing unless stated otherwise.

Sequin bag

Cut one strap and one bag shape from felt. Fold the bag shape as directed, wrong sides facing, and sew up the sides close to the edges. Sew each end of the strap to the top of the bag sides. Cut a buttonhole in the flap and sew a bead on the main bag to act as a button. Sew sequins over the front of the bag and along the strap.

Flip flops

Cut four flip flop shapes from felt. Sew two together with neat running stitch close to the edge. Cut a toe strap and sew it in place on the sole as shown on the template. Repeat for the other flip flop. Let your imagination run riot to create any decoration.

50s-style bag

Cut out the shapes from fabric and felt as directed. Fold the fabric in half and sew up the edges with a 2mm (⅛in) seam. Push in the corners and hold to finger press. Hem the short edges. Attach each end of the strap to the top of the bag, also securing the top corners of the bag. Slip stitch the flap along the top back edge. Cut a buttonhole in the flap, sew a bead on the bag, and button it up.

Two-tone mules with knitted straps

First make two straps. Using 2¾mm (US 2) needles and 4-ply yarn, cast on 10 sts. Work 2 rows in K1, P1 rib. Cast off.

Cut out four sole shapes, two from pink felt and two from white. Sew a pink and a white shape together with running stitch, securing each end of a strap on opposite sides of the sole. Repeat for the other mule.

Yellow knitted mules

First make two soles. Using 2¾mm (US 2) needles and 4 ply yarn, cast on 14 sts. Work 14 rows in st st. Cut the yarn. Remove the sts from the needle. Thread the yarn through the sts, gather them up and tie off the yarn to make the toe end. Fold the knitting into three across the cast-on edge and sew up the edges.

For the mule uppers, cast on 2 sts. Beg with a K row, work in st st. Inc 1 st at each end of this and every alt row until there are 12 sts. Cast off.

Attach an upper to the sole of each mule, matching the centre of the cast-on edge of the upper with the toe end of the sole.

Drawstring dolly bag

Cut a 15 x 7.5cm (6 x 3in) rectangle of fabric. Fold the fabric in half widthways. Sew a seam down each side of the bag, starting 2.6cm (1in) down from the top edges. Press the seams and open edges flat. Sew running stitch along the open edges on the sides.

Turn under 6mm (¼in), then 2cm (¾in) along both top edges to make the drawstring casing. Sew in place. Turn the bag right sides out. Thread braid or twisted yarn through the casing. Tie to secure the ends.

Retro Pink Floral Polo Knit

An exuberant woollen country garden party piece

WHAT YOU NEED 1 x 50g ball of 4-ply yarn in brown (B) • 1 x 50g ball of 4-ply yarn in cream (C) • Scrap of 4-ply yarn in raspberry pink (R) • Pair 2¾mm (US 2) needles • 3 safety pins • Round-ended needle • 6 press studs

TENSION 30 sts x 38 rows to 10cm (4in) over st st using 2¾mm (US 2) needles

ABBREVIATIONS *See p.12*

CHART NOTE Enlarge the chart on p.124 on a photocopier for ease of reading. Read it from right to left on odd numbered (K) rows and from left to right on even (P) rows, stranding the yarn at the back of the work.

METHOD

Using R, cast on 60 sts.
Row 1: *K1, P1; rep from * to end.
Rep the last row 5 times more.
Change to colours B and C.
Next row: Following the patt on the chart and beg on a K row, cont in st st for 26 rows.
Shape armholes: K11, turn and work on these sts in st st for 14 rows.

Shape shoulder: Cast off 4 sts, P to end (7 sts). Break yarn and slip sts onto a safety pin.
Rejoin yarn to rem sts. Cast off 8 sts, K22 including st used to cast off and turn. Cont on these sts for 5 rows.
Next row: K4, turn and work st st for 9 rows. Cast off.
Return to rem sts. Slip first 14 sts onto another safety pin. Rejoin yarn, K4, turn. Cont in st st for 9 rows. Cast off.
Return to rem sts. Rejoin yarn, cast off first 8 sts, K to end.
Cont on rem 11 sts for 15 rows.
Shape shoulder: Cast off 4 sts, K to end. Break yarn and slip sts onto a safety pin.
Polo neck: With right sides facing, join shoulder and side seams.
Rejoin colour R. Knit across 7 sts on left back from last safety pin; pick up and K 8 sts down to sts on safety pin; K across 14 sts from second safety pin; pick up and K 8 sts up right front; K across 7 sts on right back from safety pin (44 sts). Work in K1, P1 rib for 8 rows. Cast off in rib.

TO MAKE UP

Sew six press studs at equal intervals down the back opening.

DD Diva

Elegant and wealthy, Princess
DD Diva has everything – beauty,
charisma, style, a wonderful sense
of humour – and, quite bizarrely,
she's also an Olympic diving
champion! Her wardrobe, aptly
named DD's Desirable Deco,
reflects her character. Beautifully
she parades her own style around
all places exotic and paradisiacal.

DD's Desirable Deco
Flamenco Frill Top, Floral Hat, and Flares • Flared Denim Strides, Calypso Sarong, and Chic Beret • Go Paradise Travel Bag • Two-tone Mules • Chunky Drawstring Bag • Rainbow Ribbons Twosome • Hoody and Cossie Combo

Flamenco Frill Top, Floral Hat, and Flares

Eclectic mixed-knit co-ordinates

WHAT YOU NEED 1 x 50g ball of multi-coloured 4-ply sock yarn or various scraps of different coloured 4-ply yarn (knit in random stripes throughout) • Pair of 2¾mm (US 2) needles • Scraps of felt for the flower motifs • Round-ended needle
For the flares: Small remnant of baby cord or similar • Basic sewing kit • Pattern paper

TENSION 30 sts x 38 rows to 10cm (4in) over garter st using 2¾mm (US 2) needles

ABBREVIATIONS *See* p.12

HAT METHOD
Crown
Cast on 17 sts. K 5 rows.
Next row: Dec 1 st at each end.
Rep the last 6 rows once more.
K 3 rows.
Next row: Dec 1 st at each end.
Rep the last 4 rows until there are 5 sts rem.
Next row: Dec 1 st at each end. Cast off.
Make another 3 pieces the same.
Join one curved edge of each piece to a curved edge of the next panel, leaving the cast-on edges open.

Hat brim
Cast on 7 sts. K 2 rows.
Next 2 rows: K5, turn, K back. Rep the last 4 rows until the shorter edge of the brim fits around the cast-on edges of crown. Cast off.

TO MAKE UP
Neatly join the short ends of the brim. Sew the brim to the hat. Cut and sew on the felt flowers, using the template on p.121.

FLAMENCO FRILL TOP
Starting with the back, cast on 100 sts.
Work in k1, p1 rib for 6 rows. K 10 rows.
Dec row: K2tog all along the row (50 sts).
K 8 more rows.
Dec row: K2tog all along the row (25 sts)*.
Cast off. Work front as back up to *.
Shape front straps: Cast off 2 sts, K4 including st used to cast off, turn and work on these sts for 30 rows. Cast off.
Rejoin yarn, cast off 13 sts, K to end.
Next row: Cast off 2 sts, work on rem 4 sts to match the other front strap.

TO MAKE UP
Join the side seams. Tie the straps around the back of the neck.

FLAMENCO FLARES

Make the trousers as the flares on p.72.
Then make the two identical flared frills
as follows:
Cast on 30 sts. St st 20 rows.
Next row: K2tog all along. Cast off.

TO MAKE UP

Stitch one frill to the bottom hem
of each trouser leg.

If you can't find sock yarn, which stripes
as it knits up, simply keep changing to
different colours as you knit. *See* p.20
for details on adding colours. In this
way you can design your own colourway.
Just remember that the yarn must be
a similar weight to knit up correctly.

Flared Denim Strides, Calypso Sarong, and Chic Beret

Spangly sequin-detailed flares, baby-cord beret, and stylish sarong get set to jet set

WHAT YOU NEED Fine-weave fabric for the sarong • Scrap of denim for the flares • Small fabric remnant for the frill • Short length of 6mm (¼in) elastic • Small scrap of baby cord for the beret • 1 button • Lace or braid trim • Basic sewing kit • Pattern paper

NOTE All seams are 6mm (¼in) and stitched with right sides facing unless stated otherwise.

DENIM FLARES METHOD

1 Enlarge the templates on p.111 to 167 per cent. Cut out two back and two front pieces from the denim.

2 Align the outside and inside leg seams of each pair of back and front pieces. Sew up the seams.

3 Turn one trouser leg right side out. Pull the other leg over it, right sides facing, and sew up the gusset seam.

4 Make a 1cm (⅜in) casing all around the waist edge, leaving an opening for the elastic. For further instructions *see* p.25.

Thread the elastic through the casing, tie it to secure, and oversew the opening to close. Sew sequins to the waist edge.

5 For the frills, cut two pieces of fabric, 23 x 7.5cm (9 x 3in). Make a 6mm (¼in) hem along one long edge of one frill. Sew gathering stitch along the opposite edge. Draw up the thread to match the hem of the denims. Sew the frill to the hem of one leg, right sides facing. Make the other frill in the same way.

SARONG METHOD

Cut a 15cm (6in) square of fabric. Stitch a 6mm (¼in) double hem around the edges.

BERET METHOD

1 Cut six pieces of cord from the template on p.115, enlarging as specified. Match and sew up the side seams of each piece to its neighbour.

2 Sew a button to the centre point. Attach lace or crocheted braid around the brim, leaving a long end to tie at the back.

Extra Babe Things

This little felt travel bag, perfect for those jet-setting moments, is made from felt remnants and an old zip.
From the felt, cut two 11 x 8cm (4⅜ x 3¼in) rectangles and a 38 x 4cm (15 x 1½in) strip. You will also need to cut from felt four corner pieces, two handles, a label, and an aeroplane motif, using the templates on p.121. Also cut an old zip to a length of 10cm (4in).

Referring to the photograph, embroider the label and then, with running stitch, attach it, two corner pieces, and the aeroplane to one of the rectangles of felt. Sew the other corner pieces to the rectangle for the back.

Cut a 10cm (4in) slit in the strip of felt, half way along its length and along the centre of its width. Carefully insert the zip.

Sew the strip in place around the perimeter of both rectangles with running stitch, securing the handles at the top of the case.

These diminutive two-tone yellow knitted mules add a darling addition to DD's wardrobe.
Make two the same, using 4-ply yarn and 2¾mm (US 2) needles. First make the soles. Cast on 14 sts. St st 13 rows. Next row: P2tog all across. Next row: K2tog, K to last 2 sts, K2tog. Break the yarn, thread it through the stitches, and gather them up. Fold the sole into three across the cast-on edge and sew up the edges.

To make the mule uppers, cast on 2 sts. Beg with a K row, work in st st. Inc 1 st at each end of this and every alt row until there are 10 sts. Next row: K4, K2tog, K4. Cast off. Sew the upper to the sole along the side edges, matching the cast-on edge of the upper with the toe end of the sole.

Mix remnants of coloured double knit cotton yarn to create a chunky feel to this drawstring bag.

This bag has some extra details to make it special – a picot edge, eyelets, and a bobble. Using 3¼mm (US 3) needles, cast on 26 sts. Work in garter st for 40 rows, adding the stripe detail by changing colours occasionally. On 41st row, work the eyelets as follows: K1, (K2 tog, yf, K1) to last st, K1. Garter st 2 rows. To work the picot cast-off edge: Cast off 1 st, *cast off 6 sts, transfer the st on the right needle to the left, cast on 3 sts; rep from * to end. Finish off. Join the back seam. Twist or plait lengths of cotton yarn to make the drawstring. To work the bobble: Cast on 5 sts, garter st 5 rows, slip all sts over the top of the first one. Cut the yarn with an end long enough to sew running stitch around the outside edge of the bobble. Pull up the thread and sew it to the drawstring. Thread the drawstring through the eyelets and tie the ends.

Seek out sequins of all colours and shapes to embellish the clothes that you make.

You can turn a pair of wide-legged jeans into disco-fever flares with the addition of a few sequins, sewn on with fine cotton thread, to make a spangly belt. The sequins will also hide any stitches around the top of the jeans.

It would also be fun to completely cover a fabric or knitted top in sequins for a ravishingly decadent get up.

To work sequins into a knitted item, first work out how many sequins you need. For complete coverage, count the total number of stitches. Then, before you start knitting, thread the required number of sequins onto the yarn. Incorporate each sequin, flat onto the right side, as you knit each stitch.

Rainbow Ribbons Twosome

Zippy little pants-and-top number in jaunty, beachy stripes – perfect deck gear

WHAT YOU NEED Worn-out pair of children's leggings, skirt, or similar with an elastic waistband • Basic sewing kit • 6mm (¼in) elastic

NOTE All seams are 6mm (¼in) and stitched with right sides facing unless stated otherwise.

TOP METHOD

1 Cut a 23 x 7.5cm (9 x 3in) piece of the waistband part of the leggings or skirt, pinning the elastic to secure it.

2 Match the two short edges and sew up the back seam.

3 Hem the un-elasticated edge with machine zigzag or hand-sewn blanket stitch.

4 To make the straps, cut two 5 x 1.5cm (2 x ⅝in) strips of the same fabric. Fold them in half lengthways and sew around the edges, leaving an opening for turning.

5 Turn right sides out and sew up the opening. Adjust the length of the straps on the doll and and attach the ends to the elasticated edge of the bodice.

PANTS METHOD

1 Enlarge the template on p.111 to 167 per cent. Cut out the four pattern pieces.

2 Align the outside and inside leg seams of each pair of back and front pieces. Sew up the seams.

3 Turn one trouser leg right sides out. Pull the other leg over it, right sides facing, and sew up the gusset seam.

4 Make a 1cm (⅜in) casing all around the waist edge, leaving an opening for the elastic. For further instructions *see* p.25. Thread the elastic through the casing, tie it to secure, and oversew the opening.

If you don't have any suitably worn-out clothes to chop up, you can make this twosome out of any jersey or cotton fabric. To make the top you will also need a 20cm (8in) length of 1cm (⅜in) wide elastic. Cut out two 10cm (4in) squares of fabric. Sew up the side seams. Turn under a casing to suit the width of your elastic. Sew the casing in place and then thread in and secure the elastic. Hem the top and attach the shoulder straps as before.

You could also design a baseball cap, using the pattern for the beret on p.115 and adding a felt peak to one side out of the brim – it would certainly complement DD's range of designer gear!

Hoody and Cossie Combo

Personalized warm separate with co-ordinated cool cossie

WHAT YOU NEED FOR HOODY

1 x 50g ball of 4-ply yarn in soft blue (B) •
Scrap of 4-ply yarn in off-white (W) • Pair
2¾mm (US 2) needles • Round-ended needle

TENSION

30 sts x 38 rows to 10cm (4in)
over st st using 2¾mm (US 2) needles

ABBREVIATIONS   *See p.12*

METHOD

Back

Cast on 38 sts in W.

Work 2 rows in simple rib as follows:

Row 1: K2, *P2, K2; rep from * to the end.

Row 2: P2 *K2, P2; rep from * to the end.

Work the stripe detail: Change to B and
work 2 more ribbed rows. Change back
to W and work 2 more ribbed rows.
Change back to B and, beg with a K row,
continue in st st for 30 rows. Mark each
end of the last row to denote the beginning
of the armholes.

Next row: Inc 1 st at each end (40 sts).
Work st st for 5 more rows.**

Rep the last 6 rows until there are 46
sts, ending with inc row. Work st st for
3 rows more.

Divide for neck: K14, turn and work on
14 sts for the right shoulder.

Right shoulder: P2tog, P to the end (13 sts).

Next row: Cast off 6 sts, K to last 2 sts,
K2tog (6 sts).

Next row: P. Cast off.

Left shoulder: Rejoin yarn to inner edge
of rem 32 sts. Cast off 18 sts, K to the
end (14 sts).

Next row: P to last 2 sts, P2tog (13 sts).

Next row: K2tog, K to the end.

Next row: Cast off 6 sts, P to the end (6 sts).

Next row: K. Cast off.

Front

Work as for back up to **, at the same
time incorporating the "D" pattern from
the chart on p.125.

Divide for front opening: Inc in first st,
K18. Turn and work on 20 sts for the
left front.

Left front: St st 5 rows.

Next row: Inc in first st, K to the end
(21 sts).

Next row: St st 5 rows.

Next row: Inc in first st, K to the end
(22 sts).

When working right front (RF) only:
P 1 row.

Shape neck: Cast off 6 sts, P to end
(16 sts).

Next row: K to the last 2 sts, K2tog (15 sts).

Next row: P2tog, P to the end.

Rep last 2 rows once more (12 sts).

Shape shoulder: Cast off 6 sts, K to end (6 sts).
Next row: P.
Cast off.
Right front: With RS facing, rejoin yarn to the inner edge of rem 21 sts.
Cast off 2 sts, K to the last st, inc 1 (20 sts).
Now work as for left front noting the changes for the right front and reversing the shaping.

Sleeves

Make two sleeves alike. First join the front and back shoulder seams.
With right sides facing and using B, pick up and K38 between the markers.
Beg with a P row, st st 45 rows.
Work the ribbed cuffs as follows:
Row 1: K2, *P2, K2; rep from * to the end.
Row 2: Changing to W, P2, *K2, P2; rep from * to the end. Work 6 more rows in the stripe pattern as for the back.
Cast off.

Hood

With right sides facing, rejoin B to the right front neck, and pick up and K50 around the neck edge.
Next row: P.
Next row: K7, (K1, M1, K3) 10 times, K3 (60 sts).
St st 37 rows.
Shape hood back: K28, (K2tog) twice, K28 (58 sts).
Next row: P.
Next row: K27, (K2tog) twice, K27 (56 sts).

Next row: P.
Cont to dec as for the last two rows, working 1 st fewer on successive rows until 48 sts rem. Cast off.

TO MAKE UP

Join the side and sleeve seams.
Fold the cast-off edge of the hood in half and sew up the ends.

WHAT YOU NEED FOR COSSIE

1 x 50g ball of 4-ply yarn in turquoise • Pair of 2¾mm (US 2) needles • Round-ended needle

TENSION 28 sts x 38 rows to 10cm (4in) over garter st using 2¾mm (US 2) needles

ABBREVIATIONS *See p.12*

METHOD

Back
Starting at the gusset, cast on 6 sts.
K 1 row.
Inc row: K1, M1, K to last st, M1, K1.
Rep the last row until there are 26 sts.
Work 30 rows in garter st *.
Cast off.

Front
Work as for back to *.
Next row: P.
Next row: K2tog, K to last 2 sts, K2tog (24 sts)
Rep last 2 rows until there are 18 sts
Next row: P.
Shape right shoulder strap: K6, turn and

work on these sts only for the right strap. P2tog, P2, P2tog.

** **Next row:** K4.

Next row: K1, P2, K1.

Rep last 2 rows until the strap measures 7.5cm (3in). Cast off.

Shape left shoulder strap: Rejoin yarn to rem sts. Cast off 6 sts, K to end.

Next row: P2tog, P2, P2tog.

Work as for right shoulder from **

Cast off.

TO MAKE UP

Join the side seams and sew up the gusset seam. Cross the straps at the back and attach to the back edge, 2.5cm (1in) in from the side seams.

You could add bobble ties to the hoody. Twist or plait two lengths of yarn to make ties. Make two bobbles (*see* the drawsting bag on p.75) and attach one to one end of each tie. Sew the other end of each tie to opposite sides of the neck opening.

Make a rug for DD to bathe on by knitting a 15 x 7.5cm (6 x 3in) rectangle in stocking stitch and medium-weight yarn. Add the "D" pattern if you wish. Work a border in a contrasting colour by knitting a 2cm (¾in) strip of garter stitch to the same length as the four edges. Weave in the loose ends and then slip stitch the band in place.

Flo Tilly

Delicate dancer Flo Tilly is a star at the barre. Flo pirouettes her way through life in her own inimitable style – dressing up in her tutu to perform her jeté with cloud-like grace, dressing down in the schoolhouse to relax and practise her moves with fellow ballet stars and friends. She works with grace and fervour at her pas glissé and pas de chat, and her endurance certainly pays off as she's the star of the show in all the school galas.

Ballet Wraps
Fairisle Sloppy • Knitted Net Tutu • Pink Wrap-over Knit • Slinky Sweat Band • Floaty Bias Ballet Skirt • Ballet Slippers • Simple Stripy Slouchers • Floral Ballet Case

Fairisle Sloppy

Floppy, sloppy, fairisle jumper for warm up and relax down

WHAT YOU NEED FOR JUMPER

1 x 50g ball of 4-ply cotton in mauve (M) •
Scraps of 4-ply cotton in red, white, and
black • Pair of 2¾mm (US 2) needles •
Round-ended needle

TENSION
30 sts x 38 rows to 10cm (4in)
over st st using 2¾mm (US 2) needles

ABBREVIATIONS
See p.12

CHART NOTE
Read the chart on p.122
from right to left on odd numbered (K)
rows, and from left to right on even (P) rows,
stranding the yarn at the back of the work.

METHOD

Working back and front alike and using M,
cast on 35 sts. Work in simple rib as follows:

Row 1: K1, * P1, K1; rep from * to end.
Row 2: P1, * K1, P1; rep from * to end.
Rep the last 2 rows once more.
Beg with a K row, work 3 rows in st st.
Work Rows 8 to 13 from the chart.
Next row: Cont in st st for 13 rows.
Shape armholes: Cast off 2 sts at beg
of next 2 rows (31 sts).
Next row: K1, sl1, K1, psso, K to last
3 sts, K2tog, K1 (29 sts).
Next row: P.
Rep last 2 rows until there are 15 sts.

Shape the neck: Work 4 rows in simple
rib as follows:
Row 1: P1, * K1, P1; rep from * to end.
Row 2: K1, * P1, K1; rep from * to end.
Rep last 2 rows once more.
Cast off.

Sleeves

Make two alike, working in M. Cast on
25 sts. Work the ribbed cuff as follows:
Row 1: K1, * P1, K1; rep from * to end.
Row 2: P1, * K1, P1; rep from * to end.
Rep the last 2 rows once more.
Inc row: K, inc 1 st at each end (27 sts).
Next row: P.
Inc row: K, inc 1 st at each end (29 sts).
Cont in st st for 3 rows, ending on a P row.
Rep the last 4 rows once more (31 sts).
Next row: Beg with a K row, cont in st st
for 26 rows.
Shape raglan top: Cast off 2 sts at beg
of next 2 rows (27 sts).
Next row: K1, sl1, K1, psso, K to last
3 sts, K2tog, K1 (25 sts).
Next row: P.
Rep last 2 rows until there are 11 sts.
Next row: K1, * P1, K1; rep from * to end.
Next row: P1, * K1, P1; rep from * to end.
Rep last 2 rows once more.
Cast off.

TO MAKE UP

Using mattress stitch (*see* p.19), join
the raglan and neckband seams.
Join the side and sleeve seams.
With sleeves facing inwards and right sides
facing, stitch the sleeves in place around
the armholes. Turn right sides out.

It's easy to design your own fairisle.
Work out a pattern on graph paper
using coloured pencils to match your
choice of yarn and work out a repeat
pattern over as many rows as you like.

Knitted Net Tutu

Frothy, net confection for pirouette perfection

WHAT YOU NEED 1 x 50g ball of 4-ply cotton yarn in baby pink • 50 x 25cm (20 x 10in) netting in pink • Pair of 3¼mm (US 3) needles • Basic sewing kit • Round-ended needle

TENSION 23 stitches x 32 rows to 10cm (4in) over st st using 3¼mm (US 3) needles

ABBREVIATIONS See p.12

METHOD

Tutu pants

Make two the same. Beginning at the bottom edge of the tutu, cast on 6 sts.
Row 1: P.
Inc row: K1, M1, K to last st, M1, K1.
Rep last 2 rows until there are 16 sts.
Work 3 rows straight.* Cast off.

Tutu back

Cast on 6 sts and work as for pants to *.
Cont in st st for 28 rows.**
Shape shoulder straps: Work 2tog at each end of next 2 K rows (12 sts).
Next row: P.
Next row: K6, turn.
Strap: P2tog, P to end (5 sts).
Next row: K to last 2 sts, k2tog (4 sts).
St st 4 rows straight.
Cast off.

Rejoin yarn to rem 6 sts and make second strap to match the first.

Tutu front

Work as tutu back up to **.
Shape shoulder straps: K3 and turn.
Cont to work on 3 sts for 8 rows. Cast off.
Rejoin yarn and cast off 10 sts.
Work on the last 3 sts to make the right strap match the left. Cast off.

TO MAKE UP

Sew up the gusset and side seams of the pants, leaving openings for the legs.

Sew up the shoulder and side seams of the tutu, leaving openings for the armholes. Fold the net in half lengthways. Sew up the back seam, with a 6mm (¼in) allowance.

Sew gathering stitch around the folded waist edge and gather up the thread so that the net fits around the bottom edge of the tutu. Sew it in place. Sew the pants in place under the net. Trim the edges of the net.

You could make the skirt separately. Fold the net in half lengthways and stitch a 1cm (⅜in) casing along the folded edge. Sew the back seam up to the casing. Thread elastic through the casing and pull it up to fit the doll's waist. Tie the ends, turn in the raw ends, and oversew the opening closed.

Pink Wrap-over Knit

Cosy wrap top for warm ups and cool downs

WHAT YOU NEED 1 x 50g ball of 4-ply cotton yarn in baby pink • Pair of 3¼mm (US 3) needles • Round-ended needle

TENSION 23 sts x 32 rows to 10cm (4in) over st st using 3¼mm (US 3) needles

ABBREVIATIONS *See p.12*

METHOD

Work the back and front as one piece.
Cast on 28 sts.
Beg with a K row, work st st for 24 rows, marking each end of the 9th row.
Shape neck: K9, cast off next 10 sts, K to end (18 sts).
Next row: P9, turn and work on these sts for left front.
*St st 3 rows.
Left front: Inc 1 st at neck edge on next 19 rows, marking side edge of the 15th row (28 sts). St st 4 rows. Cast off*.
Right front: With wrong side facing, rejoin yarn to rem sts, P to end.
Work as left front, reversing the shaping, from * to *.
Rib band: With right sides facing, pick up and K52 sts from the cast-off end of the right front around the neck edge to the cast-off end of the left front.
Work K1, P1 rib for 2 rows. Cast off.

Sleeves

Make two the same.
With right sides facing, pick up and K28 sts between the markers on the back and front.
Work 10 rows in st st.
Next row: K2tog, K to last 2 sts, K2tog (26 sts).
Cont to work in st st for 9 more rows.
Work K1, P1 rib for 2 rows. Cast off.

Ties

Make two alike. Cast on 28 sts. Cast off.

TO MAKE UP

Sew up the side and sleeve seams and attach one end of each tie to the lower edge of each front.

To make the sweatband, measure around the doll's head and cut a piece of old jersey t-shirt to that size x 5cm (2in), plus 6mm (¼in) all around for seam allowances. Fold the band in half lengthways, wrong sides facing, and sew the raw edges together, leaving an opening. Turn the band right sides out and oversew the opening to close. You could also make matching legwarmers in a similar way.

Extra Babe Things

All these items can be made from scraps of old fabrics – t-shirts, dresses, oddments of felt, old beads, remnants of yarn – even the zip on the ballet bag was taken from a child's worn-out coat and cut down to size.

For this ballet skirt, cut a 81 x 18cm (32 x 7in) piece of floaty fabric on the bias, instead of along the grainline. Sew the short edges together, allowing a 6mm (¾in) seam.

Make a casing (*see* p.25) for the elastic and then thread the elastic through it. Sew on a velvet ribbon as a waist tie.

Turn up a double hem and sew on a felt flower, using the template on p.121 for the ballet bag.

For pas glissé or pas de chat, knit these perfect miniature ballet slippers in 4-ply yarn.

Make two the same. Beg at the toe end of the upper and with 2¾mm (US2) needles, cast on 3 sts. Working in st st, inc into first and last stitch on every K row until there are 11 sts. Continue in st st for 3 more rows. (K2tog) twice, K3, (K2tog) twice. Cast off.

For the soles, cast on 15 sts. St st 4 rows. Cont in st st, dec 1 st in the middle of every K row until there are 11 sts, end with a P row. (K2tog) twice, K3, (K2tog) twice. Cast off.

To make the ties, cut six lengths of yarn, measuring 40cm (16in). Plait three lengths together and knot to secure each end.

To make up the slippers, sew the uppers to the soles, matching the cast-on end of each upper to the narrow end of the sole. Sew the middle point of a tie to the back of each slipper.

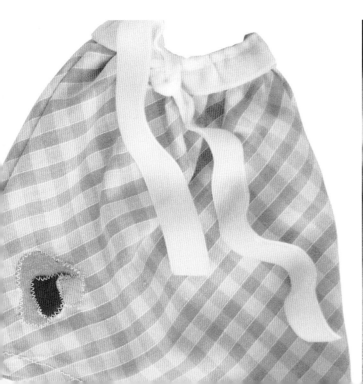

These simple, but effective slouchers are made from an old t-shirt.

You will need a 40 x 28cm (15¾ x 11in) piece of cotton jersey or old t-shirt (or enough scraps) and a length of 6mm (¼in) elastic. Enlarge the pattern on p.111 to 167 per cent. Cut the four pieces out of the jersey.

Matching the fronts and backs, sew 6mm (¼in) seams along the inside and outside legs. Turn one leg right sides out and slip it inside the other. With right sides are facing, stitch along the front and back gusset seams. Turn right sides out.

Turn over a 10mm (⅜in) casing around the waist edge. Stitch it in place, leaving an opening for the elastic. Cut a length of elastic to fit the waist and thread it through the casing. Join the ends securely and stitch the opening closed.

Little fingers will adore this tiny felt ballet case with its zipper, handles, and flower motif – they just won't be able to put it down!

Transfer to 200 per cent, then cut out all the felt shapes, using the templates on p.114.

With embroidery thread, hand sew the flower motifs from p.121 to the circle for the front of the bag, adding a bead for decoration.

Cut the slit in the edging strip and sew the zip in place. Then sew the band around the front and back circles, catching in the handles at the top, half way along the length of the zip. With the zip open, sew up the short seam at the base of the bag. Zip up the bag.

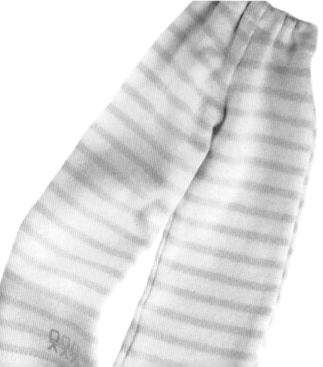

Rudy Ranch

Western wild 'n' free is red-haired, freckle-faced Rudy. The golden girl from the Big Country is as sweet as a rose bud. A rodeo rider and country girl with a flare for fringed fashion, Rudy enjoys the great expanses and wildness of the open plains. She bunks down in a modest timber shack, all gingham and homespun quilts, and spends her time riding and grooming her pony, Ranger.

Get-up
Ye-Hah Hat, Waistcoat, Flares, and Shirt • Ranch Skirt •
Cowgirl Boots • Rodeo Hat • Rosette Knit • Cow Pants • Cosy Sleeping
Bag • Cowgirl Print Denims • Saddle Picnic Basket • Floral Ho-Down Gown •
Homely Woollen Stole • Dolly Bag

Ye-hah Get-up

Hat, waistcoat, flares, and shirt make up this riding combo

WHAT YOU NEED Fat quarter of check fabric for the shirt • Bias binding to contrast with shirt fabric • Scrap of retro fabric for the flares • Scraps of hide-coloured felt for the hat • Scrap of felt for the star • 6mm (¼in) elastic • Basic sewing kit • Pattern paper • Sewing machine with zigzag stitch

NOTE All seams are 6mm (¼in) wide and stitched with right sides facing unless stated otherwise.

HAT METHOD

1 Copy or transfer the templates on p.113. Cut the shapes from hide-coloured felt.

2 Zigzag the back seam of the crown side. Starting at the back seam, carefully zigzag the brim to the crown side, easing the pieces into position. Zigzag the back seam of the brim. Oversew the crown top in place by hand.

CHECK SHIRT METHOD

1 Copy or transfer the pattern on p.118.

2 Fold the fabric in half and pin the pattern pieces to it. Cut out the pieces and transfer the markings to the fabric.

3 Turn in and sew a 3mm (⅛in) hem along the opening edges of both front pieces. Fold both pieces along the fold lines. Press the hems and folds.

4 Sew both front pieces to the back piece along the shoulder seams and press.

5 Sew the collar pieces together along the straight edges. Trim the corners and turn right sides out. Press under the raw edges. Slip stitch the collar onto the neck edge of the shirt. Top stitch, close to the outer edges of the collar.

6 For the sleeve, sew up the underarm seam. Press. Cut bias binding to go round the bottom edge of the sleeve, adding seam allowances. Sew the two short ends of binding together. Press it in half lengthways and top stitch the two ready-folded edges to the sleeve. Turn back the cuff. Sew the sleeve into the armhole, matching the seams. Repeat for the other sleeve.

7 Fold under a double 3mm (⅛in) hem around the bottom edge of the blouse and sew in place. Press.

WAISTCOAT METHOD

1 Photocopy or transfer the pattern on p.112. Cut the shapes as directed.

2 Zigzag the back, shoulder, and side seams. Zigzag up both front edges as decoration.

3 Cut a 3mm (⅛in) fringe along the bottom edge. Zigzag the pocket in place, leaving the top edge open.

TROUSERS METHOD

1 Enlarge the pattern for three-quarter length flares on p.111 and cut out the pieces.

2 Sew each front piece to a corresponding back piece, along both the side and inside leg seams. Turn one trouser leg right side out and slip it inside the other leg, right sides facing. Sew together around the front and back seams.

3 Make a 1cm (⅜in) casing around the waist edge, leaving an opening for the elastic.

Thread elastic through the casing, tie it to secure, and oversew the opening.

4 Turn under and sew a 3mm (⅛in) hem around the bottom edge of each leg.

5 Cut two 23 x 7.5cm (9 x 3in) lengths of felt for the fringe. Snip a 3mm (⅛in) fringe along each strip. Sew fringe around the bottom hem of each leg.

6 Transfer the star motif on p121 to a scrap of felt and zigzag it in place on one leg of the flares.

Ranch Skirt, Cowgirl Boots, and Rodeo Hat

Calamity Jane rides again in gingham and felt

WHAT YOU NEED 81 x 18cm (32 x 7in) gingham • Scraps of felt for the horse motif, skirt fringe, boots, and hat • 4 pearly beads • 1 small wooden bead • 6mm (¼in) elastic • Basic sewing kit • Pattern paper • Yarn for the hat tie • Sewing machine with zigzag stitch

NOTE All seams are 6mm (¼in) wide and stitched with right sides facing unless stated otherwise.

RODEO RA RA SKIRT METHOD

1 Fold the gingham in half widthways and sew up the back seam.

2 Sew a 1cm (⅜in) casing around the waist edge (for further instructions, *see* p.25), leaving an opening for the elastic. Thread elastic through the casing, tie to secure, and oversew the opening closed.

3 Turn in and sew a 3mm (⅛in) hem along the edge of the skirt. Cut a length of felt to match the circumference of the hem. Snip a 3mm (⅛in) fringe and sew the fringe around the bottom edge of the skirt, so that it falls below the hemmed edge.

4 Transfer the horse motif on p.120 to felt and sew it to the skirt with running stitch.

BOOTS METHOD

1 Photocopy the pattern on p.113 at 100 per cent. Cut the shapes out of felt.

2 Lay the boot fronts and backs next to each other and zigzag the front seam, easing the stitching over the toes.

3 Sew running stitch by hand around the sole, heel, and up the back of each heel.

4 Cut the buttonholes on the outside of each boot. Sew two beads on each boot to match the bead holes. Snip a fringe as before, up the back of each boot.

HAT METHOD

1 Follow the method on p.98. Add a felt rosette, using the template on p.120.

2 To make the chin tie, cut four 30cm (12in) lengths of yarn. Tape two lengths for each tie to a table. Twist the yarn until it is tight. Hold the end firmly with one hand and hold the mid-point with the other hand. Take the loose end to the taped end and let go of the middle so that the yarn twists into a cord.

3 Knot and trim the ends. Attach one end of each tie to opposite sides of the hat. Thread the loose ends through a bead and tie a knot.

Rosette Knit and Cow Pants

Fitted sleeveless rodeo jumper and pants with cowhide detail

WHAT YOU NEED Scraps of 4-ply cotton in cream, red, white, and black • Pair 2¾mm (US 2) needles • Round-ended needle • 1 pearly bead • Hook and eye • Shirring elastic for the pants

TENSION 30 sts x 38 rows to 10cm (4in) over st st using 2¾mm (US 2) needles

JUMPER METHOD

Work the back and front alike. Using 2¾mm (US 2) needles, cast on 28 sts and work in moss st as follows:

Row 1: *K1, P1; rep from * to end.
Row 2: *P1, K1; rep from * to end.
Rep last 2 rows once more.
Row 5: Beg with a K row, work in st st for 12 rows.
Shape armholes: K3, K2tog, K to last 5 sts, K2tog, K3 (26 sts).
Next row: P.
Rep last 2 rows until there are 14 sts. Work 4 rows in moss st. Cast off.

TO MAKE UP

Sew up the side seams and the right shoulder seam. Attach the hook and eye to each side of the left shoulder seam.

ROSETTE METHOD

Cast on 57 sts. P 1 row.
Next row: K2, *K1, slip this st back onto the left needle, pass the next 8 sts over the top of this st and off the needle, yo twice, K the first st again, K2. Rep from * to end.
Next row: P1, *P2tog, P into the front of the first yo, then into the back of the second, P1; rep from * to last st, P1.
Next row: K2tog to end. P one row. Cut yarn and using a round-ended needle, thread it through the remaining stitch loops and pull to tighten. Fasten off. Attach to the jumper with a bead.

PANTS METHOD

Work the back and front alike, using 2¾mm (US 2) needles and white yarn, cast on 6 sts.
Row 1: K.
Inc row: P1, M1, P to last st, M1, P1 (8 sts).
Rep last 2 rows until there are 26 sts. At the same time, on row 13, start to work the patt in st st from the chart on p.125. Cont in st st for 4 rows. Cast off.

TO MAKE UP

Sew up the gusset and side seams, leaving openings for the legs. Thread shirring elastic around the top edge and pull it up to fit the doll's waist.

You could make other styles of pants with this simple pattern by changing to garter stitch, working a rib at the waist, or adding bows or ribbon roses.

Extra Babe Things

This cosy sleeping bag is easy to make out of any fabric for any of the dolls, but particularly suits Rudy's lifestyle.

You will need 38 x 36cm (15 x 14in) of fabric for the outer bag and the same for both the inner bag and the lightweight wadding, plus two short lengths of tape.

Lay the wadding on a flat surface and place the two fabrics on top, right sides facing. Pin and sew around all the edges through all three layers, leaving an 8cm (3in) opening in the short base edge. Turn the fabrics right sides out and oversew the opening closed.

Fold the bag in half lengthways with the outer fabric facing and oversew along the bottom and three-quarters of the way up the side. Attach a short length of tape on each side of the opening to make a tie.

If you keep your eyes open, you will often find the ideal fabric, full of character for the right doll. This print is so "cowgirlish" – it's perfect for Rudy!

This denim print struck just the right note for a pair of rugged denims for Rudy. To make them, follow the instructions for Dot's Board Cords on p.38.

Instead, you could always make use of a worn-out pair of jeans. Choose the best bits of fabric and cut out the jeans using the templates on p.111. You could even salvage the small pockets or some of the stitching or studs for a little extra detail.

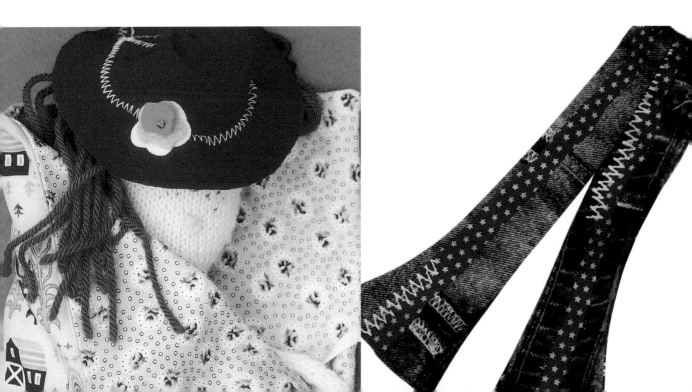

Make baskets and bags out of scraps for your dolls.

Back and front alike, using 2¾mm (US 2) needles cast on 21 sts then (K1, P1) 4 times, P5, (P1, K1) 4 times.

Row 2: (P1, K1) 4 times, K5, (K1, P1) 4 times.

Repeat last 2 rows twice more, then the 1st row once more.

Row 8: K7, (P1, K1) 4 times, K6.

Row 9: P7, (K1, P1) 4 times, P6.

Repeat last 2 rows twice. Patt 1 row. Next row patt 7, mark position for handles, patt 7, mark position for handles. Cast off.

To make up: Put both pieces together and join the side and bottom edges. Use beads for flower centres and sew on motifs from felt scraps. To make each handle, thread a large needle with 30cm (12in) of yarn and make a loop, big enough to push your little finger through, on the top edge of the basket from the 1st to the 2nd marker. Loop the yarn back to the first marker. Work buttonhole stitch along the handle until it's covered completely.

Try this floral variation on the dress theme by shortening the pattern for Bunny's Gingham Gala Gown.

Find a retro print and then follow the instructions for Bunny's gown on p.54, shortening the skirt to 15cm (6in). You could make buttonholes for armholes to ring the changes.

Homely Woollen Stole

A handknitted lacy stole, full of country charm

WHAT YOU NEED 1 x 50g ball of 4-ply cotton yarn • Pair 3¼mm (US 3) needles • Crochet hook

TENSION 23 sts x 32 rows to 10cm (4in) over st st using 3¼mm (US 3) needles

METHOD

Cast on 34 sts.

Work in patt as follows:

Row 1: K1, *(yo, skpo, K1) twice, yo, skpo, (K2tog, yo, K1), twice, K2tog, yo; rep from * to last st, K1.

Row 2: P17, K1, P to end.

Row 3: *K1, (K1, yo, skpo) twice, K2tog, yo twice, skpo, K2tog, yo, K1, K2tog yo; rep from *, ending last rep yo, K2.

Rows 4 and 10: P9, K1, P15, K1, P to end.

Row 5: K3, *(yo, skpo, K1) twice, K1, (K2tog, yo, K1) twice, K3; rep from *, ending last rep yo, K3.

Rows 6 and 8: P

Row 7: K3 *(K1, yo, skpo) twice, (K2tog, yo, K1) twice, K4; rep from *, ending last rep yo, K4.

Row 9: K5, *(yo, skpo, K2tog, yo) twice, K8; rep from * to *, ending last rep K5.

Row 11: K1, (yo, skpo, K3, yo, skpo, K2, K2tog, yo, K3, K2tog, yo) twice, K1.

Rows 12 and 20: P17, K1, P to end.

Row 13: K1, (K2tog, yo twice, skpo, K2, yo, skpo, K2tog, yo, K2, K2tog, yo twice, skpo) twice, K1.

Rows 14 and 18: (P3, K1, P11, K1) twice, P2.

Row 15: K1, (yo, skpo, K2tog, yo) 8 times, K1.

Row 16: P5, (K1, P3) 7 times, P1.

Row 17: K1, (K2tog, yo twice, skpo, K1, K2tog, yo, K2, yo, skpo, K1, K2tog, yo twice, skpo) twice, K1.

Row 19: K1, (yo, skpo, K2, K2tog, yo, K4, yo, skpo, K2, K2tog, yo) twice, K1.

Row 21: K1, (K3, K2tog, yo, K1, K2tog, yo twice, skpo, K1, yo, skpo, K3) twice, K1.

Row 22: P9, K1, P15, K1, P to end.

Row 23: K1, (K2, K2tog, yo, K1, K2tog, yo, K2, yo, skpo, K1, yo, skpo, K2) twice, K1.

Row 24: P.

Row 25: K1, (K1, K2tog, yo, K1, K2tog, yo, K4, yo, skpo, K1, yo, skpo, K1) twice, K1.

Row 26: P.

Row 27: K1, (K2tog, yo, K1, K2tog, yo, K1, K2tog, yo twice, skpo, K1, yo, skpo, K1, yo, skpo) twice, K1.

Row 28: P9, K1, P15, K1, P to end.

Repeat rows 1–28 twice more.

Cast off.

To finish: Add a fringe of seven or eight tassels across the top and bottom edges of the stole. For each tassel, cut six 4cm (1½in) lengths of yarn. Fold the bundle of six in half and use a crochet hook to pull the loop of the tassel through the knitting. Then bring the loose ends of the tassel through the loop and pull to tighten.

Dolly Bag

This drawstring bag, with its carry straps, will keep your doll safe and clean, and give you plenty of room for all her wardrobe. You could make it before you start the dolls and use it to keep your knitting and fabrics together.

WHAT YOU NEED Two 62 x 23cm (24 x 9in) rectangles of patterned fabric and two the same size of lining (main bag) • 14cm (5½in) diameter circle of patterned fabric and the same of lining (base) • 41 x 3cm (16 x 1¼in) of patterned fabric (border) • 41 x 3cm (16 x 1¼in) patterned fabric cut on bias (piping) • 41cm x 7mm (16 x ¼in) piping cord • 1m (40in) cotton tape • Basic sewing kit • Safety pin

NOTE All seams are 1cm (⅜in) wide and stitched with right sides facing unless stated otherwise.

METHOD

1 Place the two pieces of patterned fabric for the main bag right sides together. Mark the position of the drawstring casing at two points on each long side, 4.5cm (1¾in) and 5.5cm (2¼in) from the top edge. Sew the seams on the long sides, leaving an opening between the markers. Turn right sides out.

2 With right sides facing, sew the short ends of the border strip together. With wrong sides together, fold and press the border in half lengthways. Press under 6mm (¼in) along both long edges. Sew the border, catching both edges and aligning the seams, around the top edge of the main bag.

3 With right sides facing, sew the short ends of the bias strip together. Join the ends of the piping cord with a few stitches to form a loop. Fold the bias band in half lengthways, wrong sides facing, and baste it in place over the cord.

4 Aligning the seams and raw edges, pin and baste the piping around the bottom edge of the main bag. Turn the bag inside out.

5 With right sides together, pin the patterned fabric base to the bottom edge of the main bag, clipping notches into the seam allowance as necessary to ease the fabric. Hand sew it in place or use a zipper foot if machine sewing.

6 Make the lining as for the main bag, leaving an opening at the bottom of one seam for turning and omitting the piping. With right sides facing, fit the lining inside the bag, matching the side seams. Sew it to the main bag around the top edge.

7 Turn the bag right sides out through the opening in the lining. Oversew the opening closed.

8 Draw two parallel lines on each side of the bag to join the markers for the casing. Sew two rows of running stitch along the lines. Thread the tape through the casing with a safety pin. Sew the raw ends together and secure them to the bottom of the bag.

You could embroider the doll's name on the bag to make a very special gift. Choose a fabric that will display your embroidery well and have fun with the colours and stitches.

Patterns & Templates

Use the patterns and templates on the next few pages to make the sewn garments and accessories, following the instructions given here and in each project.

Where possible, the patterns and templates are printed at the correct size, but some will need to be enlarged on a photocopier, for which the appropriate enlargement factor is given. Where a pattern is printed at less than the full size, maximum length and width measurements have been given so that you can check easily if you have enough fabric.

Photocopy the patterns or templates you need and either use the print-out to cut out the fabric or trace the images onto pattern paper or thin card first. All the heavy, solid lines are cutting lines, the dashed lines represent sewing lines, and dotted lines are for folds.

The patterns allow for a 6mm (¼in) seam allowance unless stated otherwise. Always align the arrow on the pattern with the straight grain of the fabric so that the garment will hang properly.

GOWN

For Bunny's Sparkly Ribbon-tied Gown, you need fabric and lining for just the Bodice Front. For her Flower Power Mini, you need the Bodice Front and Backs.

Enlarge the pattern pieces to 143 per cent.

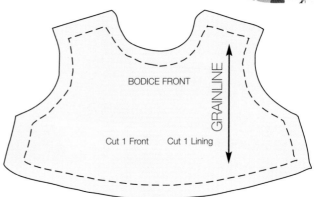

BODICE FRONT

GRAINLINE

Cut 1 Front   Cut 1 Lining

Max length = 11½cm (4½in)   Max width = 7cm (2¾in)

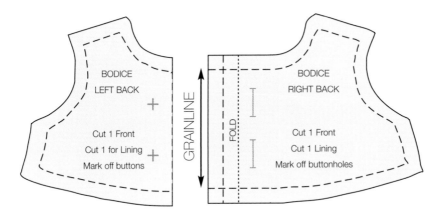

BODICE
LEFT BACK

Cut 1 Front
Cut 1 for Lining
Mark off buttons

GRAINLINE

FOLD

BODICE
RIGHT BACK

Cut 1 Front
Cut 1 Lining
Mark off buttonholes

TROUSERS AND SHORTS

Use this pattern at its full
length for Dot's Board
Cords and Flo's Slouchers.
Use the three-quarter length
for Rudy's Ye-hah Flares
and DD's Flamenco Flares
and Flared Denim Strides.
For DD's Stripy Pants,
use the template at the
shorts length.

Enlarge the pattern
pieces to 167 per cent.

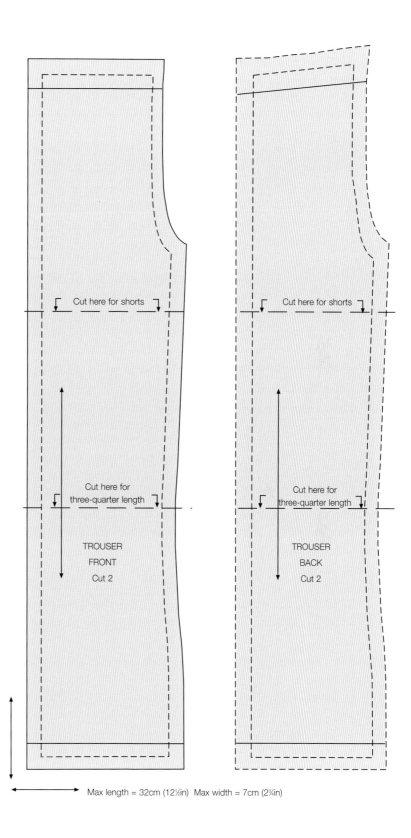

Cut here for shorts

Cut here for shorts

Cut here for
three-quarter length

Cut here for
three-quarter length

TROUSER
FRONT
Cut 2

TROUSER
BACK
Cut 2

Max length = 32cm (12½in) Max width = 7cm (2¾in)

WAISTCOAT

There is no need for a
seam allowance here –
simply lay the edges
next to each other and
zigzag them together.

Cut out the pattern
pieces at 100 per cent.

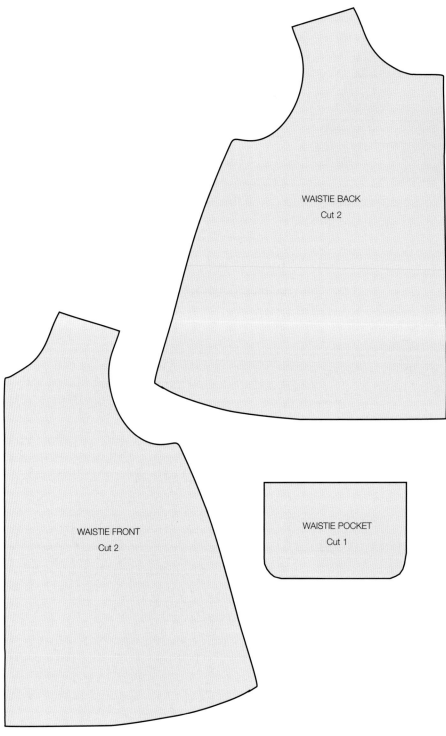

WAISTIE BACK
Cut 2

WAISTIE FRONT
Cut 2

WAISTIE POCKET
Cut 1

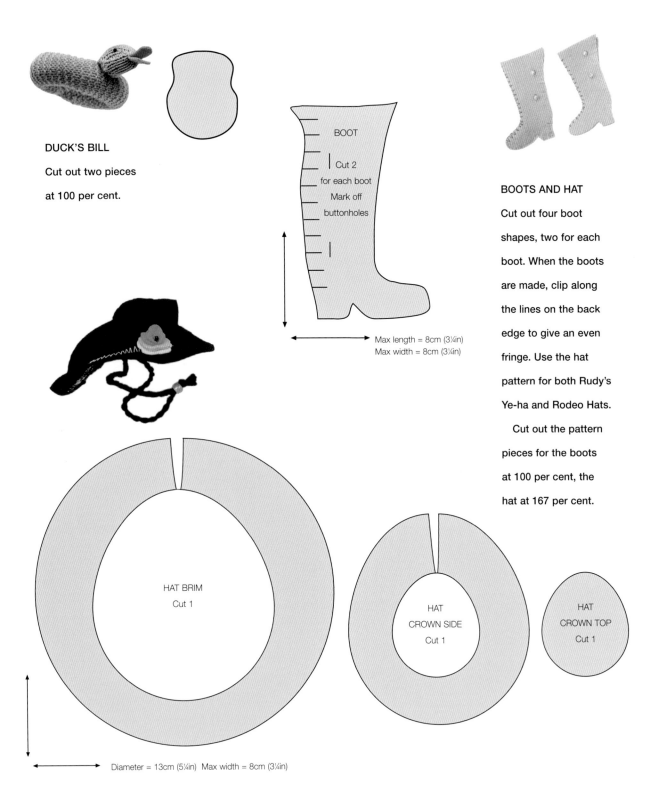

DUCK'S BILL

Cut out two pieces

at 100 per cent.

BOOT

Cut 2
for each boot
Mark off
buttonholes

Max length = 8cm (3¼in)
Max width = 8cm (3¼in)

BOOTS AND HAT

Cut out four boot

shapes, two for each

boot. When the boots

are made, clip along

the lines on the back

edge to give an even

fringe. Use the hat

pattern for both Rudy's

Ye-ha and Rodeo Hats.

Cut out the pattern

pieces for the boots

at 100 per cent, the

hat at 167 per cent.

HAT BRIM
Cut 1

HAT
CROWN SIDE
Cut 1

HAT
CROWN TOP
Cut 1

Diameter = 13cm (5¼in) Max width = 8cm (3¼in)

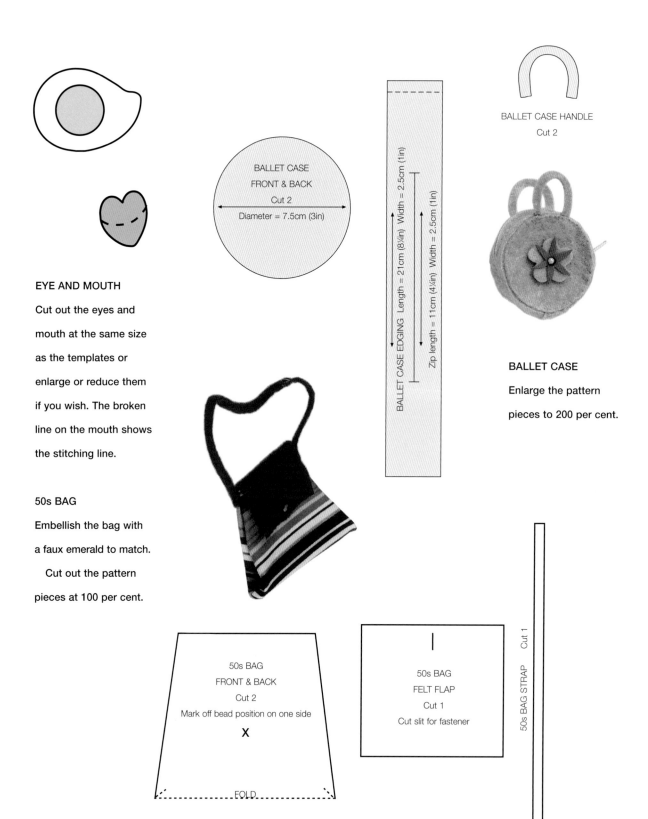

BALLET CASE
FRONT & BACK
Cut 2
Diameter = 7.5cm (3in)

BALLET CASE EDGING Length = 21cm (8¼in) Width = 2.5cm (1in)

Zip length = 11cm (4½in) Width = 2.5cm (1in)

BALLET CASE HANDLE
Cut 2

EYE AND MOUTH

Cut out the eyes and
mouth at the same size
as the templates or
enlarge or reduce them
if you wish. The broken
line on the mouth shows
the stitching line.

BALLET CASE

Enlarge the pattern
pieces to 200 per cent.

50s BAG

Embellish the bag with
a faux emerald to match.

Cut out the pattern
pieces at 100 per cent.

50s BAG
FRONT & BACK
Cut 2
Mark off bead position on one side

X

FOLD

50s BAG
FELT FLAP
Cut 1
Cut slit for fastener

50s BAG STRAP   Cut 1

SEQUIN BAG

Cut out the template
and fold the felt along
the dotted lines as you
would an envelope.

Cut out the pattern
pieces at 100 per cent.

SEQUIN BAG STRAP   Cut 1

I

- - - - - - - -
FOLD

SEQUIN BAG
Cut 1

FOLD
- - - - - - - -

Mark off bead position
Cut slit for fastener

X

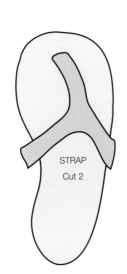

STRAP
Cut 2

FLIP FLOPS
Cut 4

FLIP FLOPS

Pair up the soles and
sew them together
with running stitch.

Cut out the pattern
pieces at 100 per cent.

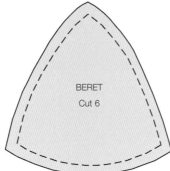

BERET
Cut 6

BERET

Sew the pieces together
like a patchwork,
leaving the bottom
edges open. Attach
a button to the top.

Enlarge the pattern
pieces to 143 per cent.

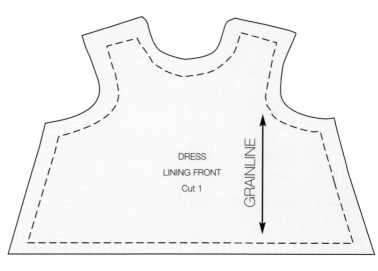

DRESS
LINING FRONT
Cut 1

GRAINLINE

DRESS

You need two fabrics
for Bunny's Psychedelic
A-line – one retro print
and a lining.

Enlarge the pattern
pieces to 143 per cent.

DRESS
FRONT
Cut 1

GRAINLINE

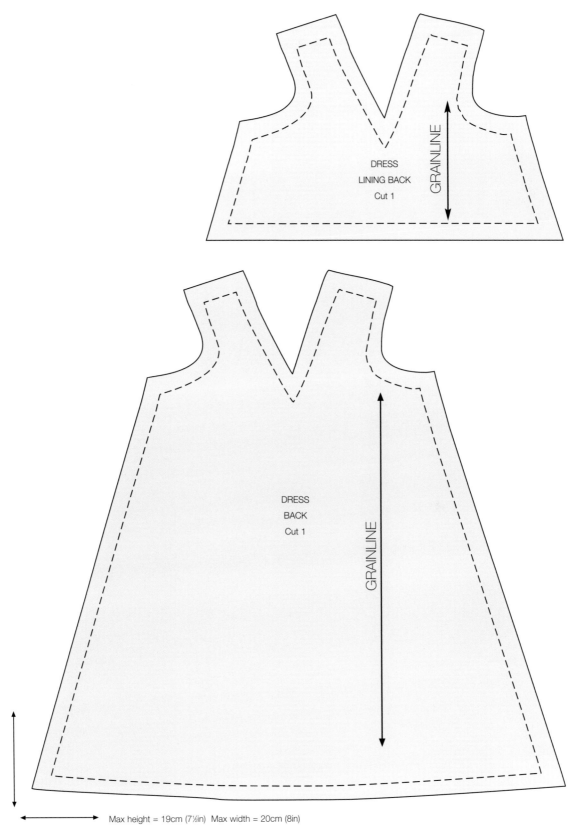

DRESS

LINING BACK

Cut 1

GRAINLINE

DRESS

BACK

Cut 1

GRAINLINE

Max height = 19cm (7½in) Max width = 20cm (8in)

BLOUSE AND SHIRT

Use this pattern, without the Collar Stand, for Rudy's Ye-hah Shirt. You do not need the Sleeve for Dot's Sleeveless Seersucker Blouse.

Cut out the pattern pieces at 100 per cent.

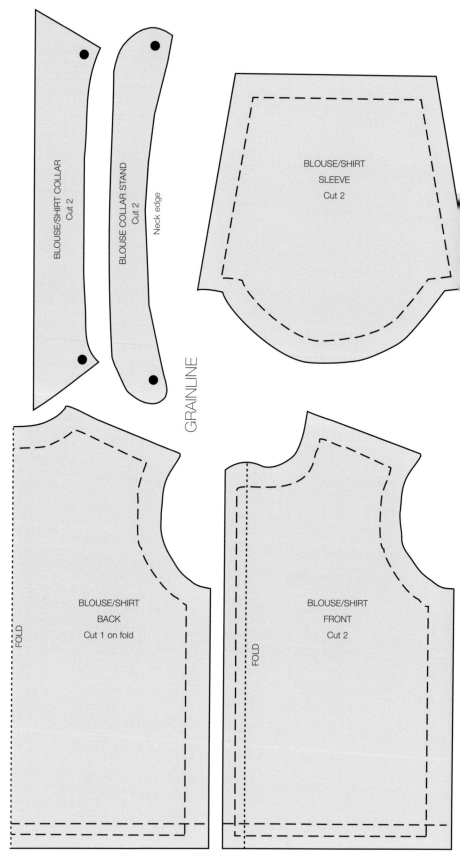

BLOUSE/SHIRT COLLAR
Cut 2

BLOUSE COLLAR STAND
Cut 2

Neck edge

GRAINLINE

BLOUSE/SHIRT
SLEEVE
Cut 2

BLOUSE/SHIRT
BACK
Cut 1 on fold

FOLD

BLOUSE/SHIRT
FRONT
Cut 2

FOLD

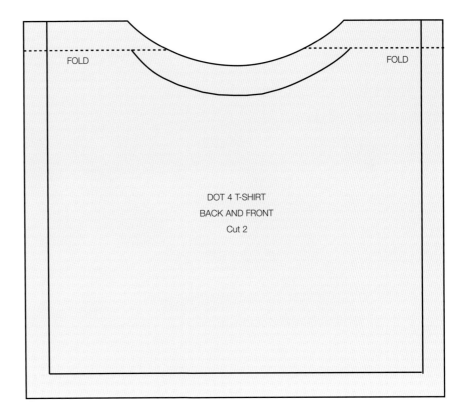

DOT 4 T-SHIRT

If you want to patch the fabrics for this t-shirt, do that first and then cut out the pattern pieces. A scrap of jersey with hand embroidery adds to the charm.

Cut out the pattern pieces at 100 per cent.

DOT 4 T-SHIRT
SLEEVE
Cut 2

FOLD

FOLD

DOT 4 T-SHIRT
BACK AND FRONT
Cut 2

Motifs

Whether it's for Dot's Board Cords or DD's suitcase, you can transform scraps of felt into nearly instant decoration that will make all the difference to your babe's street cred.

Use the motifs on these pages to embellish the doll's garments and accessories – each one bestows a special touch of femininity, cheeky charm, or humour. You can add more gorgeous or glitzy detail by combining different colours of felt, working some embroidery stitches, or attaching fabulous beads.

If you're feeling adventurous, have a go at designing your own funky motifs.

Cut the motifs out of felt at 100 per cent. Note that some of them combine layers of different shapes, each one in a different colour. Felt is ideal for these tiny adornments because it comes in lots of lovely colours,

doesn't fray, and doesn't need binding, giving you much more scope for creativity.

The motifs must be attached securely, but a single stitch or an outline of running stitch is usually all it takes to hold them in place. For Bunny's butterfly slippers, use two long stitches along the centre of the butterfly to define its body. A single stitch in the centre will attach any of the flowers and stars, although you could attach a central bead at the same time, for example for Flo's Ballet Case or Rudy's Rodeo Hat.

Attach the horse and saddle to Rudy's Ranch Skirt with running stitch. Use the same around the plane on DD's Go Paradise Travel Bag, but work a few longer stitches to detail the cockpit and the wording on the label before attaching them.

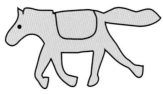

Knitting Charts

The charts on the following pages are for the patterned knitted garments for Dot, Bunny, DD, and Flo.

Each square on a chart represents one stitch; each row of squares a row of stitches. The striped squares represent ribbing. The charts are numbered down both sides. Odd or knit rows are numbered on the right, even or purl rows on the left. Read the charts from right to left for knit rows, then left to right for purl, from bottom to top.

FAIRISLE SLOPPY

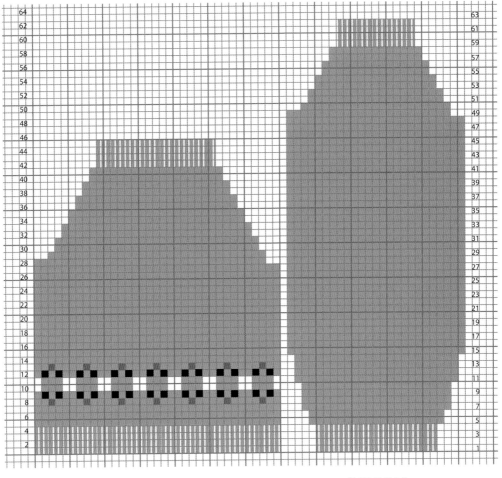

FRONT AND BACK Knit 2   SLEEVE Knit 2

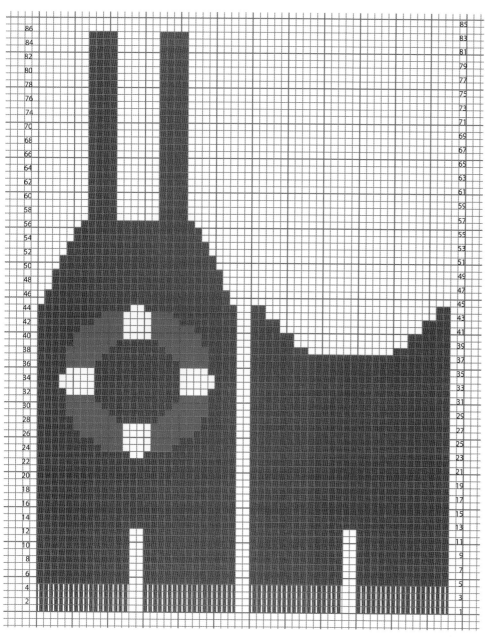

FRONT   BACK

LIFESAVER BATHER

When you reach row 23, begin working in the lifesaver ring motif. Start the white yarn at the beginning of the row, stranding it across at every third stitch. Knit 13 sts in red, introduce the white and knit 2 sts, then drop the white and knit another 13 sts in red.

RETRO PINK POLO

Begin with a rib and
then work the pattern
by stranding the
unused yarn across
the back of the work.

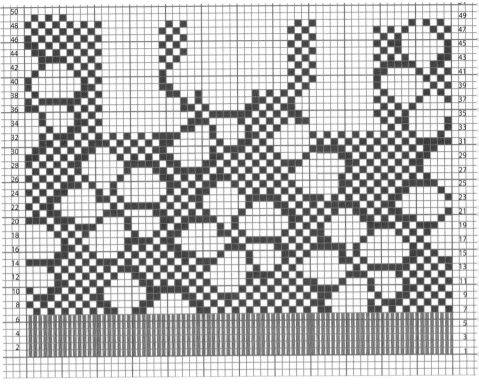

FRONT AND BACK Knitted in 1 piece

BLUE BUBBLES KNIT

The bubble pattern is
worked just on the left
sleeve and right front.

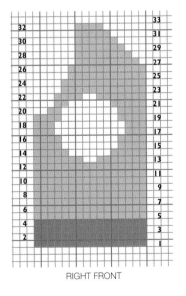

RIGHT FRONT

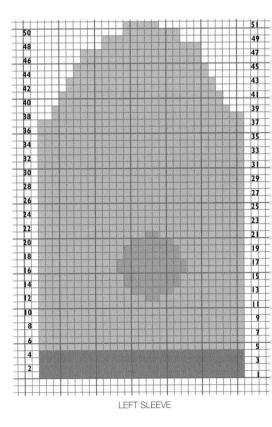

LEFT SLEEVE

COW PANTS

Start knitting in the pattern on row 13 of the pants.

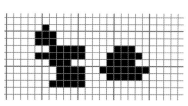

FRONT AND BACK

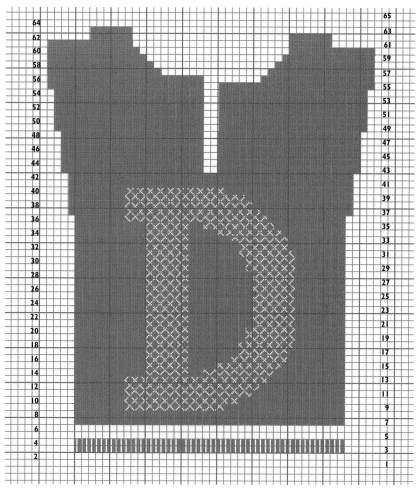

FRONT

D HOODY

Knit the "D" motif only on the Front. On row 9 knit to the point where the motif starts, purl 14 sts for the first row of the "D", and then knit the rest of the row. On the next row, work purl as usual, but knit the stitches across the motif. Continue in this way to "reverse out" the "D" until the motif is complete.

KEY

knit on RS rows
purl on WS rows

purl on RS rows
knit on WS rows

Babes' Care

Taking pride in your wonderful creation is as important as the process of making it.

The joy of making something so entirely gorgeous and lovable as the babes and their wardrobes from items of old clothing and other remnants is immense. Not only will you have made something out of nothing, you will also rekindle the special spirit and memories associated with treasured items such as your child's first dress or your favourite cashmere. If you do need to use any new fabrics, remember to wash them before use to avoid shrinkage later.

To keep your work clean until it is complete, store it in a clean bag or pillowslip. Alternatively, the Dolly Bag on page 108 will give your work perfect protection until it is needed to carry one of the babes.

Carefully wash by hand any recycled fabrics with special finishes. Otherwise, ordinary cottons and jerseys can be washed on a normal 40-degree spin wash.

Take a look at any yarns bands that are available to check special washing instructions for the knit. Most modern wools and cottons can be washed on a low-temperature spin wash, or certainly by hand. Dry the knits flat, away from direct heat, re-shape them while damp, and then very lightly steam or press them.

Index

Page numbers in **bold** refer to projects

A

accessories
  for ballet 93
  beach gear 45, 46, 81
  duck ring 46, 113
  rug 81
  shawls 54, 106–7
  sleeping bag 104
  stole 106–7
  templates 113
  towel 45
  see also bags

B

babes
  Bunny Bright **50–65**
  caring for 126
  DD Diva **66–81**
  Dot Pebbles **32–49**
  Flo Tilly **82–93**
  making *see* making the babes
  Rudy Ranch **94–107**
bags
  ballet case 93, 114
  basket 105
  beach bag 45
  dolly bags 62, 108, 126
  drawstring bags 62, 75, 108
  sac bag 56
  shoulder bags 62, 114, 115
  templates 114–15
  travel bag 74
buttons/buttonholes 25, 36, 44

C

clothes
  for ballet 85–92, 93
  beach gear 35–49, 76, 78, 80–1
  blouses 36, 98, 118
  cardigan 40–1, 124
  dresses 48, 105
  gowns 54, 58, 110
  hoody 78, 124
  jumpers 64, 86–7, 90, 102, 122, 124
  knickers 60, 102

knitting charts 122–5
mini dresses 59, 60, 110, 116–17
sarong 72
shirts 36, 98, 118
shorts 76, 111
skirts 38, 92, 100
swimsuits 42–3, 46, 78, 80–1, 123
t-shirt 44, 119
tops 70, 76
trousers 38, 71, 72, 92, 98, 104, 111
tutu 88
underwear 60, 102, 125
waistcoat 98, 112

E

embroidery stitches
  French knots 25, 28
  Swiss darning 20
equipment 8, 22
eyelets 21, 75

F

fabrics 10
  binding 22
  fat quarters 22
  felt 10, 28, 120
  washing 126

H

hats
  bandannas/headbands 36, 60, 90
  baseball cap 76
  beret 72, 115
  cowboy hats 98, 100, 113
  floral 70
  for special occasions 55
  swim hat 45

K

knitting charts
  abbreviations 12
  enlarging 40, 42, 64
  for fairisles 87, 122
  for patterned clothes 122–5
  reading 40, 42, 64, 87, 122
knitting needles 8

knitting stitches
  garter stitch 6, 15
  knit stitch 15
  moss stitch 16
  purl stitch 15
  stocking stitch 6, 15
knitting techniques 12–21
  adding new colours 20, 43, 71, 123, 124
  casting on and off 14, 17
  decreasing 17, 21
  holding needles and wool 13
  increasing 16
  knit 15
  picking up stitches 18
  purl 15
  ribbing 16, 122
  seams 19
  sewing up 19, 26
  shaping 16, 21
  skpo 21
  starting off 13
  stranding 20
  tension 10
  texture 16, 125
  turning rows 16
  yo or yf 21
knots
  French knot 25, 28
  slip knot 13

M

making the babes 26–31
  body 26
  facial features 28, 114
  hair 30
motifs 119, 120–1, 123

P

pockets 24, 112

S

safety issues 30, 57
selvedge 22
sewing patterns 23, 110–19
  dots 22
  enlarging 23, 110
  fold lines 22, 110
  grainline 22, 110
  making your own 23

transferring 23, 110
sewing stitches
  back stitch 19
  basting stitch 24
  buttonhole stitch 25
  French knot 25
  gathering stitch 22, 24
  mattress stitch 19
  running stitch 24
  slip stitch 24
  zigzag stitch 22
sewing techniques 22–5
  appliqué 22
  bias 22
  casing 25
  clipping 22
  gathering 22, 24
  glossary 22
  hems 24
  measuring up 23
  mitring 22, 24
  pinking 22, 23
  quilting 22
  seam allowance 22, 23, 110
  sewing up 23
shoes
  ballet shoes 92
  boots 113
  cowboy boots 100
  flip flops 38, 62, 115
  mules 57, 62, 74
  slippers 57, 120

T

techniques 12–25
templates 23, 28, 110–19
toy stuffing 30
trimmings 44, 54
  beads 30, 56, 120
  bobbles 75
  ribbon 54, 57
  sequins 75
  straps 45, 114, 115
  strings 56, 62, 75
  tassels 107
  ties 81, 90, 92, 100
  see also motifs

Y

yarns 10, 26, 30, 126

Acknowledgments

I would like to thank Anna, Tim, Christine, and Catherine at Mitchell Beazley, as well as Karen and Marilyn – you are all brilliant. Also my mother, Wendy, for helping with the knitting of the seemingly endless arms, legs, and bodies.

Babes, similar to the ones featured in this book, are available as a knit kit – visit www.dotpebbles.com; and for stockists of yarns similar to those used in the book visit www.knitrowan.com.